SHORT LIFE

SHORT
LIFE

Living for What Matters
During our FEW DAYS on Earth

Michael Edward Nichols

NASHVILLE

NEW YORK • LONDON • MELBOURNE • VANCOUVER

SHORT LIFE
Living for What Matters During our FEW DAYS *on Earth*

Published in New York, New York, by Morgan James Publishing. Morgan James is a trademark of Morgan James, LLC. www.MorganJamesPublishing.com

ISBN 978-1-64279-971-2 paperback
ISBN 978-1-64279-972-9 eBook
Library of Congress Control Number: 2019920517

Cover Design by:
Rachel Lopez
www.r2cdesign.com

Morgan James is a proud partner of Habitat for Humanity Peninsula and Greater Williamsburg. Partners in building since 2006.

Get involved today! Visit
www.MorganJamesBuilds.com

DEDICATION

To Precious Jewels
And to all my children, grandchildren, and students

IN MEMORY OF

Calla Woods	9 years on earth
Cindy Zucca	17 years on earth
Sam VanGieson	26 years on earth
Steve Szoke	32 years on earth
Micah Wakeman	43 years on earth
Jeff Higgenson	58 years on earth
Marvin Flowers	61 years on earth
Jim Billington	72 years on earth
Janice Nichols	81 years on earth
Mina Talcott	99 years on earth

WITH SPECIAL THANKS

To my daughter Sarah Ann for helping me become a better writer and also encouraging me by telling me my book was better than _____'s book (un-named famous multi-million-copy selling author).

To my former student Jonathan Harrison for his professional copy-editing done as a gift of love.

CONTENTS

CHAPTER 1

INTRODUCTION:
THE DASH LIFE

Life is too short not to focus on the dash

"We knew everything about life except how to live it."
E. Stanley Jones

D eath clarifies everything. Indeed, thinking about our death can teach us how to live for what really matters. Linda Ellis's famous poem "The Dash" encourages people to think about the dash that will one day be carved on their tombstone. Tombstones are inscribed with two dates—a date of birth and a date of death—usually with a small dash between. What matters most is not when you were born or when you die, but how you lived during the period represented by the dash. That is what this book is about: living for what matters during the short time we have on Earth. Sometimes, when I officiate at a graveside service, I encourage participants to look about at the tombstones surrounding us. I remind them that one day, a stone will be etched with their own name. Then I challenge them to spend some time in reflection before returning to their cars and homes, examining their lives to see how they are living during the dash.

I have a friend who loves to spend time in cemeteries, especially when facing a big challenge or an important decision. She says that doing so gives her perspective. Focusing on your own death might seem morbid, but I have found it just the opposite. Death clarifies everything, helping us realign our priorities. And because the thought of death can motivate us to do the important things that we should be doing, I think we need to think about our own death more often than we do.

I started writing this book during the summer I turned 50. I am finally publishing after turning 60. Life seems to be flying by. Many times over the last few years I have thought *I need to get this book done before my life on Earth is over, or no one will ever be helped by it!* During my twenty-five years of teaching at Lincoln Christian University (LCU) in Lincoln, Illinois, I have seen students die for a variety of reasons. This book includes the stories of two LCU students who lost battles with cancer, one at age 32 and the other at age 26. Seeing the terribly short dashes on their tombstones reminds me that my own dash could end soon.

Reminders of the brevity of life are all around, sometimes even coming in the mail. I was shocked to realize how much I was aging when I received a membership application from AARP (American Association of Retired Persons) the summer when I turned 50. As I wondered why I would be receiving mail from AARP, it hit me like a ton bricks: I became eligible to be an AARP member by turning 50! Something about the number 50 intimidated me—50 felt old. Turning 50 reminded me that I was getting closer to my death—that I had fewer years left to live than I had already lived. I honestly had never thought of myself as being old before I received that letter.

I now intentionally surround myself with reminders of life's brevity. When I pick up a newspaper, I turn to the obituary page to read about people who have died after living lives shorter than my own. Doing so reminds me that I might die at any time. It also helps me think of the days and years that extend my life as being days and years of grace. In the last few years, I have lost three dear friends, one aged 43, one aged 61 and the other aged 62. I carry all three of their pictures in my day timer to remind me daily that life is short—that I have no guarantee of living a certain number of years.

For some time now, I have wanted to write a book on the only subject on which I feel qualified to write—my life. I have asked the Lord to give me a spirit of openness and transparency as I write. The writers who have influenced me most over the years have been those who have courageously shared lessons they have learned from brokenness, wounds, and struggles in their own lives. What I write comes from my own spiritual journey—from birth to 60 years old. I pray that some of these life lessons will resonate within your own soul. I also pray that you will share your own spiritual journey with others. As someone reminded me recently, our stories don't belong to ourselves. Rather, our stories belong to each other, and ultimately they belong to God, the author of life. We should all want to live well during our brief time on Earth, but we should also want to help others live well. I pray that reading this book will help you live your life for what matters, influencing others to do the same.

Every week, I try to read from the works of Henri Nouwen and E. Stanley Jones, now dead, who in their writings mentor me in my life's journey. I hope that long after I have put aside my earthly tent, a few people will still read this book. I will try my best to be authentic and transparent, writing about things I hope will strike a chord in your heart, helping you in your journey with the Lord. No one should travel through life alone—so I hope these meditations of a fellow traveler help you in your own life's journey.

Why forty chapters? Forty is a very special number in Scripture. Noah experienced forty days of rain, Moses stayed forty days on Mt. Sinai, Joshua and Caleb explored the Promised Land for forty days, Elijah was strengthened for forty days by a single meal, Nineveh was given forty days to repent, and Jesus fasted forty days in the wilderness—and appeared to his followers for forty days after his resurrection. I challenge you to take forty days—or maybe forty weeks—to explore your inner and outer worlds, deeply examining your life. You might find some giants that need slaying, as Joshua and Caleb did. And if you do, I pray you will respond, "I can do this with God's help." The ten other spies, along with most of the Israelites, didn't think that conquering the Promised Land was possible, and their doubt sent them wandering forty years in the wilderness. I pray that this book will help you build your faith so that you are ready to take the territory that God wants you to conquer in your own life on earth. I also pray that you will take this forty-day (or forty-week) challenge to think about the brevity of your life and consider how to live, during your own dash, for the things that matter.

LIFE APPLICATION

1. Write your date of birth on a card, then follow it with a dash and a question mark; highlight the dash if you like. Then put the card where you will see it every day.

2. Set aside a regular time each week or month to think intentionally about your death, perhaps in a nearby cemetery.

3. Read one chapter of this book every day for the next forty days, or every week for the next forty weeks. Find someone with whom to discuss the life application suggestions that end each chapter.

PART ONE

The *SHORT LIFE* Impacts your Inner World

CHAPTER 2

THE ALERT LIFE

Life is too short to sleep through

"Be on guard! Be alert! You do not know when that time will come."
Mark 13:33

"So then, let us not be like others, who are asleep,
but let us be alert and self-controlled."
1 Thessalonians 5:6

May 27, 2008, was a very sad day for me. On that day, Bob Szoke let people know that his son Steve's earthly journey was over: Steve had gone on to be with the Lord. Steve lost a hard-fought battle with colon cancer, dying just a few days short of his thirty-third birthday and leaving behind a wife and 7-year-old daughter. Steve had been one of my favorite students at Lincoln Christian University. He had a passion for evangelism like no one else's and had given his life to reaching people who, as he said, "fall through the cracks of life." Steve had a huge heart for at-risk youth in the Chicagoland area, and he yearned to plant a church that would welcome and disciple them. I had been praying for Steve since I first learned he had been diagnosed with cancer, but I was still shocked by an email he sent just two months before he died:

So, I'm not even quite sure how to write this. I went to bed last night and woke up today believing my doctor was going to call with good news and tell me that today was my first day of remission. Nothing could be further from the truth of the situation. I was instead called in for a consultation and told I was now in stage 4 colon cancer. Candy and I went in and were informed that these past 8 months of chemo and radiation were a complete wash and that I did not respond to the medicine at all. That I, in fact, had small cancerous nodules throughout the lining of my abdominal wall. What does that mean? He told me that I would need a new kind of chemo to combat this, that I would now be in chemo on a weekly basis and that I might be looking at 1–3 years left of my life. The one thing I did not want to hear from my doctor's mouth is him giving me days on a calendar, which is exactly what he did. I want to thank everyone for their prayers and ask them to continue to pray for me. I have no problem continuing to fight tooth and nail for my life. The one thing I have always wanted in life is to grow old with my wife (whom I love so deeply) and to be there for my child (whom I also love so deeply). This news does put things in perspective for me; how could it not? Now is the time that I need my friends and family the most. I said in a sermon this past Sunday that throughout this disease, there have been many times that I have completely collapsed under the weight and burden of everything and just asked God to carry me. My God has not abandoned me, He's just needing to carry me a little further.

One morning, I received my own wake-up call. I was in a hurry to get to work when my preschool-aged daughter, Sammy, lying on the couch in the family room, caught me just before I reached the door and yelled,

"Daddy! Would you find Barney for me on the TV?" My first thought? *Sorry kid—I'm late, and I'm outta here!* But I hesitated, decided to be a good daddy, and took an extra minute to find the channel for Barney the purple dinosaur before flying out the door. I jumped in my little red Nova and raced onto the blacktop road in front of our house—only to see a huge semi-truck lying on its side a hundred yards from our house. The accident had just happened. The driver, having clambered out of his cab, was talking to a bystander in a pickup truck, who was calling the police. Then the driver was on the phone with the police, explaining how he lost control of his rig while swerving to miss a deer. I was completely shaken—my life could have been over that morning had I not taken a minute to be a good father to my daughter. I envisioned an accident between a semi-truck and a little red Nova—the Nova lost. I reflected on this wake-up call for a long time afterward.

A dear missionary friend wrote about a wake-up call in her own life. Just a week after returning to her country of service in Southeast Asia, a 25-year-old friend of hers, whom I'll call Ruth, was killed in a truck accident, leaving behind a husband and two small sons. The news caused my own friend to fear God in her own life, realizing that she hadn't the slightest idea when God would take her home. I was moved by her challenge:

If you have something you need to do now—do it now! If you want to serve God, decide to serve him now! If you want to draw close to God—draw close to him now! If you need to repent—repent now! If you need to love those who oppose you—love them now! Tell those who are not loveable that you love them. Everything that you do, you must do it with a pure heart and a heart that loves God, because time will not wait for you. We don't know when God is going to take us or when Christ is going to return!

When I read her wake-up call, two phrases jumped off the page at me: "we don't know when" and "do it now." At times I am tempted to postpone things that the Lord is prompting me to do, but these seven words motivate me to action.

Earthly life can certainly be very short, sometimes being counted in days, not years. Several years ago, I visited with friends in Ottawa, Canada, who had lost a child a few months before. Mark and Rachel's little Joshua lived only twenty-nine days. He was their first child, as well as the first grandchild on one side of the family. Mark and Rachel were grieving deeply, but they were grieving as Christians, people who have hope beyond the grave. I found them thanking the Lord for the twenty-nine days they had with little Joshua, looking forward to seeing him again in heaven. On the other end of the spectrum about that same time, my wife, Julie, traveled to Canada to celebrate her grandmother's ninety-ninth birthday—which, as things turned out, was her last. Both a twenty-nine-day life and a ninety-nine-year life are, from God's point of view, brief. We don't know when God will call us home—so do it, whatever it is; now!

Wake-up calls are all around. Just look at the news, or even at events unfolding around you. On August 19, 2009, a tornado hit the small town of Williamsville, Illinois, near my home, leveling a Casey's convenience store and an antique store where a friend of mine worked—though fortunately she wasn't there at the time. The same tornado struck a country house just two miles from our own. That same day, a high school friend of our daughter Sammy, miraculously walked away from a serious truck accident. That day awakened me to the brevity of life. And there have been other such days, including the one when my good friend Travis told me he had hit a deer head-on while driving down the interstate at eighty miles per hour. He told me he never saw the animal—only felt the crash and the air bag deploying. Then later, while on a vacation trip in Wyoming, I, too, hit a deer head-on on the interstate. And Travis was right—I was frightened by how quickly the accident came and went.

When I was 41 years old, I began to feel as if God were trying to get my attention. That year, three different men whom I knew, all aged 41, died—one in a car wreck and two from brain aneurysms of which they had been unaware. That year, I started thinking seriously about my own mortality.

Strange how we try to constantly push our inevitable death out of our minds! I have come to believe that we must do just the opposite. If we can learn to intentionally consider our own impending death, then we change death from an enemy to be feared into a wise teacher for which to be thankful. Be alert to the wake-up calls around you so that death can teach you how to live.

LIFE APPLICATION

1. Can you remember a wake-up call that you have received? What do you think God was saying to you through it?
2. What memory triggers can you put in your life to remind you of your life's brevity and of your own mortality?
3. If you knew you had only two months to live, what would you do? What if a doctor gave you only one to three years to live?

CHAPTER 3

THE BRIEF LIFE

Life is too short not to realize how quickly it passes

"Teach us to number our days aright,
that we may gain a heart of wisdom."
Psalm 90:12

"He remembered that they were but flesh,
a passing breeze that does not return."
Psalm 78:39

T he brevity of life is a major theme in the Bible. In Psalm 39, David asks the Lord to show him his life's end and then uses three metaphors to illustrate a simple theme: Life is brief. David describes life as a mere handbreadth, a quick breath, and a fleeting phantom. Compared to an eternal God who has no beginning or end, our earthly life span seems a mere blip. When I think of life as a single breath, I'm reminded of someone blowing out a long breath on a cold morning, only to see it quickly evaporate.

Show me, LORD, *my life's end* and the number of my days; let me know how fleeting is my life. You have made my days a mere handbreadth; the span of my years is as nothing before you. Each man's life is but a breath. Man is a mere phantom as he goes to and fro: He bustles about, but only in vain; he heaps up wealth, not knowing who will get it. But now, Lord, what do I look for? My hope is in you. (Psalm 39:4–7)

These rich metaphors are set in the context of a busy person who gives no thought to the length of life. The phrase *bustles about* especially resonates with people of our time. A person can be so busy trying to get ahead that he or she fails to remember that the race might be nearly over!

Praying David's prayer might do us good. You could say that David is asking God to help him visualize his own funeral. When I read Stephen Covey's *Seven Habits of Highly Effective People*, I took his challenge to visualize my own funeral. I tried to think of who would be crying and who would be indifferent. I tried to imagine my pallbearers, as well as what various speakers would say about me. And I found that visualizing one's own funeral is an effective way of setting life goals.

The Bible is rich with metaphors about the brevity of life. In one prominent example, Moses uses the illustration of grass: "[God sweeps] men away in the sleep of death; they are like the new grass of the morning— though in the morning it springs up new, by evening it is dry and withered" (Ps 90:5–6). I have mowed grass every summer since I was in the fifth grade. Keeping up with it during the spring rains and the early summer is difficult, but by late summer, it becomes dry, brown, and dead. Paying attention to the grass could teach us something about how quickly our lives on Earth pass.

The prophet Isaiah adds another metaphor—flowers: "All men are like grass, and all their glory is like the flowers of the field. The grass withers and the flowers fall" (Isa 40:6–7). I don't know a lot about growing flowers, but I know how much my wife loves them when I bring some home to her. I also know that they can be expensive. I love the expression of joy I see on Julie's face when I give her flowers, but I hate how quickly flowers wilt and die, even when kept in water. Paying attention to flowers could also teach us something about the brevity of life.

In his turn, Job says, "My days are swifter than a runner; they fly away without a glimpse of joy" (Job 9:25). By runner, Job doesn't mean a marathon runner, methodically running twenty-six miles. Rather, think about Olympic sprinters, who finish a hundred-meter race in fewer than ten seconds.

In the New Testament, James warns those who make plans "for tomorrow":

Now listen, you who say, "Today or tomorrow we will go to this or that city, spend a year there, carry on business and make money." Why, you do not even know what will happen tomorrow. What is your life? You are a mist that appears for a little while and then vanishes. Instead, you ought to say, "If it is the Lord's will, we will live and do this or that." (Jas 4:13–15)

Think for a moment about mist, whether an early morning fog that burns off as the sun rises or the steam of a tea kettle. In either case, mist doesn't hang around for long. In chapter 1, we talked about how an entire life is represented by a single dash on a tombstone. A nihilist looks at the dash and sees no point in it, but a Christian looks at the dash and asks a stewardship question: *Because life is so brief and passes so quickly, how can I live it fully unto the Lord?*

Psalm 78 talks about God's perspective on our lives: "He remembered they were but flesh, a passing breeze that does not return." We need to ask God to help us take his view of the brevity of our lives. Because every one of us is a single heartbeat—a single breath—from our eternal home, God spends all of Scripture, both Old and New Testaments, telling us about life's brevity using a variety of metaphors. Yet we continue putting out of our minds the idea that we will die soon. Accepting the brevity of life and looking our upcoming death square in the face can teach us how to live a life of significance.

Christians must have a proper biblical theology of death. To hear some of us talk, death sounds like just about the worst thing that can happen to someone. But such a perspective is a far cry from Paul's declaration to the church at Philippi: "For me, to live is Christ and to die is gain" (Phil 1:21). As John Mott said, "Death is just a place where Christ-followers change trains." In fact, Psalm 116:15 exclaims: "Precious in the sight of God is the death of his saints!" Sir Walter Scott called death not "the last sleep," but rather the "final awakening," and he was correct: Christians should look at death the way they look at sleep. We aren't afraid to go to sleep; we fall asleep fully confident that we will rise in the morning. We should face death the same way, confident that we will wake up to an eternal morning.

Jim, an old college friend of mine, lost his dear wife. How I love Jim's perspective—his theology—concerning the death of Janetta:

I don't usually post on the wall but there are too many people to inform in a brief span of time. One of my wife Janetta's favorite Bible verses is "but joy comes in the morning." Her fight with cancer is over and there was joy in heaven this morning as she joined her earthly dad and heavenly father.

In 1 Corinthians 15:55, the Apostle Paul mocks the power of death: "Where, O death, is your victory? Where, O death, is your sting?" At Steve Szoke's visitation, I was handed a card mocking the power of cancer:

Cancer is so limited!
It cannot cripple LOVE
It cannot shatter HOPE
It cannot corrode FAITH
It cannot destroy CONFIDENCE
It cannot kill FRIENDSHIP
It cannot shut out MEMORIES
It cannot silence COURAGE
It cannot invade the SOUL
It cannot destroy PEACE
It cannot quench the SPIRIT
It cannot lessen the POWER OF THE RESURRECTION
IT CANNOT STEAL ETERNAL LIFE!

Now that is a good biblical theology of death!

LIFE APPLICATION

1. Which biblical metaphor speaks powerfully to you? Which one do you connect with, whether emotionally or visually? What practical memory trigger or symbol can you place in your daily schedule to help you reflect on life's brevity?

2. Sit down and start writing: How do you hope your funeral goes? Be as detailed as possible. Consider giving a copy of what you write to a close family member or friend.

3. Is your theology of death more cultural than it is scriptural? Spend some time thinking about how our culture views death, comparing that view on death to biblical passages that teach God's perspective on death.

CHAPTER 4

THE BELOVED LIFE

Life is too short not to feel loved

*"How great is the love the Father has lavished on us, that we
should be called children of God! And that is what we are!"*
1 John 3:1

*"Self-rejection is the greatest enemy of the spiritual life because
it contradicts the sacred voice that calls us the 'Beloved.' Being
the Beloved expresses the core truth of our existence."*
Henri J. M. Nouwen

I have not always felt loved by God. Life on Earth is brief—how sad to live it without knowing and experiencing the truth of God's love for oneself! I grew up with an emotionally abusive father who had quite a temper. I was constantly frightened that his hand would strike me or his foot kick me. I was even more afraid of his words—words screamed in anger about how stupid and incompetent I was—"Just think! Don't be so stupid!"—or the opposite: "Don't think! Just do what I tell you!" Inside, I was hearing the accusation *Mike, you are too stupid to even think.* Unknown to me, my relationship with my earthly father superimposed itself on my view of God. I have spent much of my life trying to straighten out my warped theology.

I decided to be baptized at age 9, out of fear of God's wrath. I had no problem believing that I deserved God's punishment. I assumed that God was always mad at me, just like my father was. I assumed that God was watching me, waiting for me to blow it so that he could beat me or spank me. I grew up with no mental concept of a loving father. To this day, I have no memory of my father saying the words "Mike, I love you" or "Mike, I'm proud of you." Ironically, my father, for much of his life a Christian preacher, hindered my understanding of the love of God. From a young age, I ached to please both my heavenly and earthly fathers. I quickly evolved into an obsessive "people-pleaser," exhibiting an insatiable desire for attention and approval. I loved to play basketball and was the starting point guard during my junior and senior years of high school. Once I came home after playing a great game—in which I made many assists and scored many points—thinking that my dad would praise me when we sat down for our post-game review over a meal at home. But after that game, like after so many other games, my heart sank when there was no "Great game, Mike!" As always, Dad focused only on what I did wrong in the game, pointing out all the things I needed to improve for next time.

My desire for approval has both haunted and motivated my entire life. As a missionary, I found myself working the equivalent of three full-time jobs simultaneously during my time in the DR Congo. Looking back, I now see what happened: I exhausted myself attempting to please my earthly and heavenly fathers. In fact, I came home from Africa on the verge of a nervous breakdown. My search for approval almost killed me.

I survived my transition back to the United States by slowly correcting my view of God. I became intrigued by the voice of God on two special occasions in Jesus's life. At Jesus's baptism, God the Father said, "This is my Son, whom I love; with him I am well pleased" (Matt 3:17). On the Mount of Transfiguration, Jesus heard those same words again: "This is my Son, whom I love; with him I am well pleased" (Matt 17:5). These words are a great model of what every child needs to hear from his or her father: *You are my child. I love you. I am proud of you.*

My theological distortions about my heavenly Father began to be corrected when I became a father myself. When my daughter Sarah was born, I cried out to God in desperation—I had never been a father before, and I knew that I was in over my head. We had flown to a small mission hospital a few days before my wife Julie was to deliver, and I paced the hospital compound, asking God for help. One day, reading my Bible in that hospital, surrounded by hills, I read Psalm 121:1: "I lift up my eyes to the hills—where does my help come from?" It was a question straight from my own heart. Verse 2 answers: "My help comes from the Lord, the maker of heaven and earth." I was so struck by these verses that I suggested to Julie that she repeat them over and over during labor and delivery—which she did. During this crisis in my life, God presented himself as a loving father, ready and willing to help me. Slowly, my perception of God began to change.

As my children grew older, other of my perceptions of God began changing. A deep desire began growing in my heart on Christmas mornings and on my children's birthdays: I wanted to give them a gift that would wow them when they opened it. I hoped for an excited response: "Wow! Is this for me? It's exactly what I wanted!" Slowly, I began believing that if my own earthly heart truly wanted to give my children their heart's desire, then surely my heavenly father wanted even more to do the same for his children. I began trusting in the God of Matthew 7:11, the heavenly Father who desires to "give good gifts to those who ask him."

When my son Jason was playing Little League baseball, the Holy Spirit warned me against the dangers of becoming a performance father. Jason was not an exceptionally good baseball player, but he seemed to enjoy being on the team. I tried my best to be an encouraging dad in the stands, shouting out encouragements to the little guy. If the truth be told, I think Jason closed his eyes sometimes when he swung at pitches. So I wasn't really expecting any heroics when, during one game, he went up to bat with the bases loaded. As the pitch came in, Jason swung as hard as he could at the pitch—with his eyes closed—and, much to his surprise and mine, connected with the ball and sent it flying deep into the outfield, between fielders. Little Jason chugged around the bases for a triple, with three runs batted in! I still remember the big smile on his face as he jumped up and down on the third base bag. When I put Jason to bed that night, I relived the baseball game with him. We talked about how cool it was for him to hit a triple that helped his team win the game. Then I felt a prompting from the Holy Spirit: *Be careful, Mike—you don't want to become a performance father.* I listened to the prompting and, after I told Jason how happy I was for him, I reminded him that if he had gone up to the plate and struck out while doing his best, my love for him would remain the same.

There are many kinds of fathers. Among them are abusive fathers, absent fathers, passive fathers, and performance fathers. But praise God for loving fathers! And we don't have to guess what a loving father looks like, for God has shown us in his relationship with his son Jesus, as recorded in the Bible.

I am happy to say that my relationship with my earthly father has greatly improved. God has given me the strength to forgive my dad for loving me poorly as a child. In fact, I took him out to lunch for his seventieth birthday several years ago and asked him about his own childhood. He told me that he had never had a personal relationship with his own father. I came away with a deeper realization of the pain with which my dad has lived his entire life. His own father had been a physically abusive alcoholic for most of his childhood—the classic town drunk. Dad told me stories of how, only a small boy, he was sent to the tavern to walk his drunk father home—something a little boy should never have been asked to do. Without justifying my dad's behavior toward me, I now understand where it originated. My favorite part of our lunch came when I shared with my dad how, by the grace of God, I have been able to show affection to my children, helping stop the abusive cycle in our family. A new cycle of love has begun—and my dad was very happy to hear it. I am so glad I took the chance to ask my dad about his own boyhood before he died! Life is too short to live with unforgiveness toward parents who may have not loved you well. It is also too short to live with an inadequate or twisted theology that tells you lies about God's love for you.

LIFE APPLICATION

1. How would you describe your relationship with your earthly father? Do you have a specific wound related to your own father? How has this relationship—or a wound incurred through it—affected your view of your heavenly father? Do you need to talk with a parent who has not loved you well to try to understand him or her better?

2. What theological truths have you learned from being a parent or from watching other loving parents?

3. What tangible thing can you put in your daily life (perhaps a special Scripture verse, something you carry in your pocket, or something you write on your bathroom mirror) to remind you daily of your core identity as a beloved son or daughter of God?

CHAPTER 5

THE CONFESSING LIFE

Life is too short to carry guilt and shame

*"Confess your sins to each other and pray
for each other so that you may be healed."*
James 5:16

*"In failing to confess, Lord, I would only
hide You from myself, not myself from You."*
Saint Augustine

I learned not to live with the consequences of unconfessed sin, in particular continual harassment by guilt and shame, by myself living with an unconfessed sin for many years. I committed the sin when I was a green missionary during my first term of service in the DR Congo.

I still remember walking away from Ed, a missionary colleague, the day I burned out his circular saw. I thought to myself, "You just *lied* to him. You say you are a missionary for God, but you are *nothing but a liar!*" When I had come too close to the metal frame atop which I was sawing, the saw blades hit the metal and burned out the engine. Ed, who was very protective of his tools, asked me, "Did you hit the metal frame?" Afraid of his reaction, I immediately lied. I let my lie go unconfessed for several years. But if I forgot about it for a while, then something would happen to remind me of it. I was trying hard to live a life of integrity, and I realized that my lie would keep bugging me until I confessed it. Finally, when I met Ed at a conference in the United States, I confessed the whole thing. Ed was very gracious; in fact, he apologized to me for being so gruff as to cause me to feel that I couldn't tell him the truth about damaging his tools.

I first heard the phrase "confessing life" from one of my students on a short-term mission trip to Mexico. Immediately attracted to the idea it represented, I decided I wanted to live that kind of life. Living the confessing life is not for the faint of heart. It takes a lot of guts to be transparent, vulnerable, and authentic. I will never forget hearing two lifetime missionaries to Africa speak to a group of fellow missionaries. Both were advanced in age, having given multiple decades to missionary service. I heard them speak in two different settings in two different countries and was shocked to hear the same advice from both: If you want to be an effective missionary, learn to *confess your mistakes* and express your sorrow over them. Such simple advice—yet so profound. And following it seems to be the hardest thing for an American missionary to do.

When I was a missionary in Zaire (now called the DR Congo) the churches with which I ministered held an altar call after the sermon each week, during which people came forward to kneel on a mat placed on the floor, confessing their sins in silent or audible prayer. Often the person would whisper his or her sins to one of the elders, who would lay hands on the person and pray for him or her. To me it resembled the Catholic practice of the confessional, except without the private box to sit in.

I was an imperfect missionary, and I lived among imperfect missionaries. I attended hundreds of Congolese church services during my ten-year missionary career, yet I never saw a missionary come forward at the end of a sermon to confess his or her sins—myself included. I am haunted by the thought of what could have happened for God's kingdom had missionaries lived openly confessing lives.

During the end of my family's second term of missionary service in the DR Congo, I committed what in that society was a cardinal sin. My wife and I, trying to fix up a house before leaving for the United States for a year of furlough, were having some masonry work done and were also painting some of the rooms, trying to prepare them for our return to the DR Congo. We didn't want to leave the house empty during our year in the United States, so we asked Wabalassa, a local preacher, whether he and his family would like to live in the house, rent-free, during our absence. He was elated by our offer. I encouraged him to move in but asked that he and his kids not enter certain rooms that we were still having fixed up. But whenever I stopped by to check on the carpenter's and mason's progress, they expressed their frustration about how Wabalassa's children were messing up their work.

I reminded Wabalassa not to use certain rooms yet, but his children's interference continued. After yet again hearing one of my workers describe how the kids had messed up his work, I lost it and went over to the house. When I arrived, I began yelling at Wabalassa, his wife, and his kids, my raised voice audible to neighbors on all sides: "I can't believe you let your kids mess up the work again that I've been paying to have done—especially when I am letting you live in this house for free!" I stormed out of the yard and went home steaming mad. That night I couldn't sleep as the Lord began to convict me of my angry reaction. I argued with the Lord, telling him that I was in the right and Wabalassa in the wrong. But the Lord prevailed, telling me that my response was wrong, especially in such a culture. In the DR Congo, to yell at someone in public was to bring great shame on that person—one of the worst sins you could commit against someone else.

The next Sunday, I asked to meet with Wabalassa and his wife after church. As we sat in a back room together, I humbly asked for their forgiveness, the tears flowing down my face. They forgave me, asking for my forgiveness for what had happened, also with many tears. I will never forget the cleansing feeling I had when I confessed my sin to them. Confessing not only brought healing to my heart, but also cemented my friendship with Wabalassa and his wife, making it stronger than ever. Sometimes a broken bone that heals properly can become stronger than ever at the place where it was originally broken. Similarly, confession brought healing, reconciliation, and a closer relationship.

When we try to hold our sins inside, not confessing them, we suffer emotionally and physically. In Psalm 32, David said,

When I kept silent, my bones wasted away through my groaning all day long. For day and night your hand was heavy upon me; my strength was sapped as in the heat of summer. Then I acknowledged my sin to you and did not cover up my iniquity. I said, "I will confess my transgressions to the LORD"—and you forgave the guilt of my sin. (Ps 32:3–5)

Psalm 51 is a psalm of confession. David talks about being cleansed, washed, and restored. He shares the secret to having joy and a sustaining spirit—*confession*. He knows that God's greatest desire from us is not external, ritualistic worship; rather, true worship of God consists of a broken spirit and a contrite heart.

Opinions differ about the Roman Catholic practice of confessing to a priest. But I think that Roman Catholics are onto something—confession offers something powerful and healing. I would like to extend the practice of confession using the doctrine of the priesthood of all believers. The Apostle Peter told first-century Christians that they were a chosen people, a holy priesthood. I really think we should take our priestly function with each other seriously. As priests, we serve as bridges between God and people who are hurting. We become "God with skin on": God with a touchable face. I have had the privilege of being a priest of God in several people's lives as they confessed sins to me. For example, a woman named Lisa came to me together with her husband and confessed several things that she had said against him and done to him. At the end of her confession, I put my hand on her arm and looked her straight in the eye, speaking God's truth to her: "You are forgiven *right now* for all the bad things you thought and did to your husband." The truth of God had an immediate healing effect on her and on her relationship with her husband, who had also forgiven her.

The power of temptation and addiction can be broken by dragging our sins into the light by confessing them. In spring 2005, I led a group of students on a short-term mission trip to Montreal, Quebec. Our team of ten students split up in the evenings, staying with different families from the small church with which we were working; I ended up staying with the pastor and his wife. One evening, I asked whether I could watch their television late that night to catch a University of Illinois basketball game—the Illini were progressing in the NCAA Final Four tournament. The pastor found the game for me, then went to bed. At half-time, I flipped through the channels only to happen on a channel airing a panel talk show in French. I was shocked when the show cut to scenes of explicit sex.

I wish I could say that I immediately fled back to halftime, but I ended up watching more of the pornographic show than of the basketball game. I still remember how horrible I felt later that night when I went to bed—as well as the next morning, when I awoke. I felt dirty, defeated, and worthless. I thought here I am, a *Christian* university professor on a *mission* trip, being hosted in a *pastor's* house—and I spent much of the night watching *porn*! Satan had a field day with me, shouting, "Mike, you are worthless! God doesn't love you anymore! God can't use you anymore in ministry!" The only way I was able to overcome these accusations was to confess my sin before we left—not only to the pastor, but also to the team of students I had brought to Canada. That confession was one of the most humiliating of my entire life. But God used it years later, when one of the female students who had come with me on the trip confessed to me her own struggle with pornography, telling me that my confession had empowered her to confess it to me and to others.

Can you imagine Jesus asking you one day in heaven, "Why did you keep on carrying the burden of unconfessed sin while on Earth?" Life is too short to carry unnecessary burdens of guilt and shame. It's time to fess up!

LIFE APPLICATION

1. What sins have you committed but never told anyone about? Reflect on a time when you felt free and unburdened because of confession.

2. Who do you know who would be a good "priest" for you? (This person should be trustworthy, gentle, and caring—and able to keep a confidence.) Schedule regular confessing visits with your "priest."

3. Write down on a card a Scripture passage dealing with confession (for example, Psalm 51:10 or Psalm 32:1–5) and set it where you will see it often. Write "confessing life" in a place where you will see it often.

CHAPTER 6

THE FORGIVING LIFE

Life is too short to hold a grudge

"Forgive as the Lord forgave you."
Colossians 3:13

"To forgive is to set a prisoner free and discover that the prisoner was you."
Louis B. Smedes

What kind of things would you do if you had only a few months to live? A few years ago, my friend James told me about a friend of his who found out that he had only a few months to live. James' friend created a list of people with whom he needed to reconcile, and he spent the last weeks of his life making his best attempt to mend fences. He didn't want to die with unforgiveness in his heart. His actions affected James greatly. Even though James wasn't sick, he decided to do the same thing. James listed seven people with whom he needed to reconcile, and he began reporting to me each time he crossed a name off his list. *What a great idea for everyone!*

James' list included someone who had said something bad about him, someone who had ripped him off in a lawsuit over his aunt's estate, and an uncle who—angry at James' mother—took the only piece of nice furniture James and his mother had (a trophy case that held all James' trophies). James' list also included his first ex-wife: Even though James viewed himself as the one mostly at fault for their divorce, he still felt bitterness about things she had done and said to him. The hardest person for James to forgive was his father, who had abandoned him and his mother when he was as a child and with whom James had had no real ongoing relationship. James made a serious inventory of those he needed to forgive and is well on his way to checking off everyone on his list.

Forgiveness is a major theme in Scripture. Genesis tells the story of Abraham's two sons, Ishmael and Isaac. The difficult relationship and hostility between Jews and Muslims today can be traced back to the story of these two sons. They grew up together but lived apart when Abraham sent Ishmael away. God promised to bless both of their descendants and make them both into great nations. It is interesting to read what happened with both of them when their father Abraham died. Both Jews and Muslims trace their religious heritage to Abraham. In Genesis 25, we find that "Abraham breathed his last and died at a good old age, an old man and full of years; and he was gathered to his people"—followed by an astounding sentence: "His sons *Isaac and Ishmael* buried him in the cave of Machpelah" (Gen 25:9). The death of their father actually brought them together! Death can give us an opportunity for forgiveness and closure. We don't know whether Isaac and Ishmael reconciled, but the opportunity was there. And the opportunity is still there: Jews and Muslims could still be brought to love each other for the sake of their common ancestor, Abraham.

We must learn to keep short accounts with the people we love. Indeed, while I was writing this chapter on forgiveness, real life paid me a visit. My wife Julie and I disagreed this morning about mowing our yard—and I raised my voice in anger. I see myself as being in charge of the lawn mowing, and though my wife often wants to help me with it, her help turns into her wanting to do things her way. But her way and my way have distinct differences, which has led to an ongoing argument that makes me feel disrespected as a leader (leader of the mowing!) and that makes her feel unloved, as if I don't want to do things with her. After our argument this morning, we have kept our distance from each other. But when I saw her drive off in the car by herself, I called her to ask her to come home so that we can talk things out. How the yard gets mowed isn't a big deal in the grand scheme of things, so I am asking the Lord to give me wisdom, including the right words and tone, so that I can apologize and explain my feelings without becoming defensive.

I love Ruth Bell Graham's comment: "A happy marriage is the union of two good forgivers." I ended up apologizing for raising my voice at Julie. As a side note, isn't it interesting how different people define "yelling"? If my voice holds any hint of emotion, my volume raised even a tiny bit, Julie calls that yelling. But I grew up with constant loud yelling, so I define yelling as something loud enough to make someone cover his or her ears. I was definitely guilty of loud yelling that day. My apology paved the way for the reconciliation of our relationship and another attempt to analyze what had caused our argument in the first place.

I'd like to say that I apologized easily, but apologizing continues to be one of the most difficult things for me to do. Why is it so hard to say "I am sorry" to someone? These three words are powerful when spoken sincerely and without additional "buts." There is a big difference between extending an argument and ending one. Saying "I'm sorry, but..." negates the apology. The first time I "attempted" to apologize to Julie, I felt I needed to be heard, so I said *I'm sorry, but you need to know how frustrated I was because of things you said and did.* The next morning, I was confronted by a Scripture during my morning devotions. Proverbs 12:18 says, "Reckless words pierce like a sword." I sensed a deep conviction from the Holy Spirit and realized that my words, spoken in anger, had in fact pierced my wife deeply. I am learning that it is *never appropriate* to yell at a spouse and that I should *always apologize* for that—even if I think I am in the right in our argument.

When we don't forgive someone in our heart, we end up giving that person too much power over us. One simple definition of forgiveness is giving up our right to hurt someone back. In Scripture, God declares that vengeance is his, not ours. Some use the phrase *forgive and forget*, yet doing so is humanly impossible unless God erases our memory. The good news is that we can be in a state of true forgiveness even if we remember something bad that someone did to us. The key is *not remembering it "against them."*

Forgiveness is a process rather than a one-time event. Several signs show that you have truly forgiven someone. You have forgiven someone when you can honestly pray for that person and ask God to bless him or her. True forgiveness has come when you have given up all attempts to hurt that person. Another obvious sign that the poison of resentment is gone is when you can think of the person without experiencing a sharp pain in your gut. Some think that only a complete restoration of relationship signifies forgiveness, but that is not true. You can truly forgive someone in your heart while still maintaining healthy boundaries in your relationship with a person who has proven untrustworthy.

Impending death can teach us valuable lessons and motivate us to get our priorities straight. Eddie Smith, a longtime missionary to Nigeria, wrote in her journal about life lessons she had learned during her struggle with cancer, which eventually took her life. My favorite lesson of hers was simple and profound: "Forgive *everyone* for *everything*!"

To forgive someone and give up your right to hurt them back is not an easy thing to do when the hurt is devastating. My spiritually adopted Congolese son, Tresor Yenyi, works with survivors of sexual violence in eastern Congo. The pain that has been inflicted on these young women is unimaginable, yet Tresor knows that the only real cure is forgiveness. As Tresor says, "True peace will only come in the victims' hearts when they will have forgiven their offenders." Being hurt by someone emotionally is like being stabbed with a knife; forgiveness is pulling the knife out so that you can begin to heal.

We often have great difficulty even talking about times when we were victims of someone else's sin. Satan even has a way of using shame to make us think that sin against us is somehow our fault—that we deserved it. When I was in junior high, I was sexually abused by a man who was a friend of our family—a man who was a preacher, someone to whom I looked up. But over a short period of time, he molested me sexually. His sin against me made me feel ashamed and worthless. I wasn't able to share about the abuse with anyone besides my wife until I was in my forties. Talking about it first to a counselor and then publicly has been part of my journey of total healing. I eventually came to the point of forgiving the man who abused me as a boy; now I desire to meet him again to confront him about what he did to me, to tell him that I forgive him, and to find out whether he has received help.

As much difficulty as we can have forgiving those who have hurt us, sometimes the most difficult person to forgive is our own self when we have sinned. Because Satan, the great accuser, loves to constantly remind us of our sin, we must become good at reminding Satan of God's grace in our life. A Christian man whom I know succumbed to temptation and visited a strip club in Fort Wayne, Indiana, when he was traveling by himself. He confessed his sin to the Lord and to others, but he was never able to forgive himself for what he had done. Satan continued to remind him of his sin, accusing him of it every time he read or heard the name *Fort Wayne*, bringing overwhelming feelings of shame and guilt. But then everything changed. While driving through Fort Wayne again, he experienced a time of profound healing. When Satan's accusations came and the familiar feelings of shame began to surface again, the man began to pray in exhausted desperation to the Lord—begging him to take the shame away. Deep in his heart, the man heard the Lord speaking to him: "From now on, when you hear the name *Fort Wayne*, you will no longer think of it as the city of your sin—rather, you will think of it as *the city of my grace* in your life!"

Life is too short to have unforgiveness in your heart, whether for others or for yourself. Forgive *everyone* for *everything*!

LIFE APPLICATION

1. Make a list of those whom you need to forgive. Then ask God for the strength to forgive them and the wisdom to know whom you should approach to seek reconciliation.

2. Have you ever been sinned against in a significant way about which you never told anyone? Ask the Lord for the courage to tell someone about what happened as a first step in the process of forgiveness.

3. Have you committed any sin for which you are still finding it difficult to forgive yourself? Ask God for the grace to forgive yourself.

CHAPTER 7

THE COMPASSIONATE LIFE

Life is too short not to act with compassion

"When he saw the crowds, he had compassion on them, because they were harassed and helpless, like sheep without a shepherd."
Matthew 9:36

"But a Samaritan, as he traveled, came where the man was; and when he saw him, he took pity on him. He went to him and bandaged his wounds, pouring on oil and wine. Then he put the man on his own donkey, took him to an inn and took care of him."
Luke 10:33–34

Compassion is more than feeling sympathy for someone; it requires action. The first time I felt compassion was during the summer of 1972, the summer before I started high school. I was a very selfish, self-centered 14-year-old. My dad asked me whether I wanted to accompany him to Arizona to help him hold a "Baseball and Bible" camp for Native American boys who lived on the reservations. I quickly agreed, because I had never been to Arizona, because I loved to play baseball, and because anything would be better than spending a bored summer in my small hometown, which had a population of only 800. My dad had been raising money in the Midwest to help a mission build a boarding school for Native American children. The school had purchased a large piece of ground but had built no buildings. My dad wanted to set up a temporary campground and build a baseball field so that the school could start ministering to the children at once. So our first week in Arizona, we laid out a baseball field in a meadow, cut down the outfield grass with sickles, scraped out a dirt infield using hoes, and built a backstop from wood and chicken wire. We erected rented tents to use as dormitories, we dug latrines, and we built outhouses. Another family from Ohio came out to serve as cooks. When we went onto the reservations to sign up kids for camp, we were able to get eighteen boys from three tribal groups, Hopi, Apache, and Navajo—the perfect number for two baseball teams. My older brother and I slept in the tent with the boys, and by the middle of the week, the tent was getting very rank. One morning, on awaking, I told the boy who was sleeping next to me to change his pants—he had been wearing the same pair of pants during the three days we had been playing baseball in the hot Arizona sun. He looked up at me and calmly responded, "I only have one pair of pants."

At once I felt something break inside of me—it might have been my brittle, cold heart. I had never felt biblical compassion before, had never really thought of anyone else's needs other than my own. I was like the Grinch who stole Christmas: My heart started growing bigger inside my chest. At the end of the week, I went up to my dad, a lump in my throat and tears streaming down my face, and asked, "Dad, can we take some of these boys back to Illinois to live with us?" The compassion I was feeling made me want to act, I was very serious about my request. My dad explained that although we couldn't take them home with us, there were things that we could do to help them. Biblical compassion causes you to act.

We can learn about compassion by looking at Jesus. In Matthew 9:35–36, we see that Jesus looked at people with eyes of compassion:

Jesus went through all the towns and villages, teaching in their synagogues, preaching the good news of the kingdom and healing every disease and sickness. *When he saw the crowds*, he had *compassion* on them, because they were harassed and helpless, like sheep without a shepherd.

When I think of how I normally look at crowds of people, this Scripture is convicting. When I see a bunch of people queuing in the checkout lane or waiting at my favorite restaurant, I usually don't have a vision of compassion such as Jesus had. My thoughts are more along these lines: *I wish all these obnoxious people would get out of my way so that I can do what I want to do!* The word translated *compassion* in this passage is connected to the word for bowels or intestines. In the first-century world, the bowels were the seat of emotions, much how we think of the heart. The idea is that something happens that touches you at the core of your being, causing you to act to help someone. C. S. Lewis writes about the temptation to *feel without acting* in *The Screwtape Letters* when Uncle Screwtape gives the following advice to his junior demon-in-training:

Let him do anything but act. No amount of piety in his imagination and affections will harm us if we can keep it out of his will ... The more often he feels without acting, the less he will be able ever to act, and, in the long run, the less he will be able to feel.

A concordance study of the times when Jesus felt such deep compassion reveals Jesus meeting people who had many various needs. In Matthew 20:29–34, we see Jesus having compassion for two blind men beside the road who called out to him, asking him to help them see. Jesus saw people who had physical needs and had compassion on them. Do we? In Mark 1:40–42, we see Jesus having compassion on a man with leprosy, who came and begged Jesus on his knees, asking to be made clean. The first time I noticed the word order in this text, it chilled me right down my spine. The text is clear: Jesus reached out and touched the man *before* healing him.

During our first month in the DR Congo, I began to better understand what Jesus was doing in this instance. In January 1984, my wife and I were living in the small village of Bomili in the Ituri rainforest, in the northeastern part of the country. We were taking part in a language immersion program, living with no other English speakers around. One day, the old pastor of the village asked us whether we wanted to visit the leper colony. I was surprised to hear of people nearby who had that disease. I felt in some ways as if I had been transported back to the first-century world. About a half-dozen lepers lived a couple kilometers outside the village in their own settlement. After visiting them, I understood that their biggest needs were emotional, not physical. Being outcasts from normal society, they were extremely lonely. Jesus knew that this man referred to in Mark chapter one, needed to be touched. He had been ostracized and marginalized from society because of his disease. Jesus could have healed him from a distance, but instead he touched him—*then* healed him.

Many people today are dying of loneliness. Often loneliness has nothing to do with the proximity of people—you can certainly be lonely in a crowd of people. Rather, loneliness has to do with the lack of friendship and intimacy. Nursing homes, for example, are full of lonely people. I love the saying "Let me come and sit with you so you will know you are not alone." Because of technology today, we have more methods of communication than ever before, but we suffer loneliness more than we ever have. We are high-tech but low-touch. Jesus saw the lonely and had compassion on them. Do we?

In Luke 7:11–15, we see Jesus having compassion on a woman in grief, a widow whose only son had died. When Jesus thought about the grief in this woman's heart, he couldn't walk past the funeral procession without acting. He brought her son back from the dead and returned him to his mother. Uncounted numbers of people are grieving today. Grief comes not only from losing loved ones in death, but also during any major loss in our life. One of my favorite quotes says that "all change is loss, and all loss is to be mourned."

People grieve when divorce causes loss of relationship, when they lose their job, or when a move brings about loss of friends. Jesus saw people who were grieving and had compassion on them. Do we?

How can we develop the compassionate eyes of Jesus? Remember when I was 14, helping with the Baseball and Bible camp? At that age, had I come across a newspaper whose cover story talked about poverty-stricken Native American children, do you think reading it would have developed compassion in me? I don't think so; reading a newspaper at that age means flipping to the comics or to the sports section. If I had come across a documentary on television about Native American children on reservations in Arizona, I might have watched for a few minutes and perhaps even felt a little sympathy. But I probably would have changed channels to find a ballgame. I have learned that the secret to developing eyes and hearts of compassion is to spend time with hurting people. When I got to know the Native American boys personally—eating with them, playing baseball with them, singing with them, and sleeping in the same tent—God began to melt my selfish teenager heart. My journey of compassion started at 14 years old in Arizona, and it has now taken me around the world.

If your compassion quotient is low, start looking for hurting people with whom you can spend time. They are all around you. Ask to be granted Jesus's eyes and heart, which won't allow you to walk by without acting. Life is too short not to act with compassion.

LIFE APPLICATION

1. Is your compassion quotient high, or low? When was the last time you acted with compassion? Ask Jesus to open your eyes so that you can see hurting people.

2. Who in your life suffers from physical illness, loneliness, or grief? Think of a practical action you can take to show compassionate love. Ask the Lord to show you which of your resources you can use, even now, to show compassion.

3. What can you do to intentionally spend more time with hurting people? Ask the Lord to give you the courage to step out of your comfort zone and into the life of someone who is hurting.

CHAPTER 8

THE LEARNING LIFE

Life is too short to stop learning new things

"Instruct a wise man and he will be wiser still;
teach a righteous man and he will add to his learning."
Proverbs 9:9

"Let the wise listen and add to their learning."
Proverbs 1:5

A few years ago I spent seven years of my life earning a Ph.D. The Ph.D. has been called a "terminal degree," but I take issue with that. I did learn a great many things on that seven-year journey— but mostly I learned how much I still didn't know. I was able to answer some questions along the way, but even the answers just raised more questions. One of the reasons why I think that heaven will never be boring is that we will always have more to learn. God created us to be inquisitive, thinking, analytic learners. And how sad it is when people stop learning! Because we were made to be lifelong learners, we should use every minute of our brief lives on Earth to keep learning new things. In fact, when we die, we just transfer to a new school.

Yogi Berra once said, "You can observe a lot just by watching." And you certainly can. The key is your attitude about learning. Many people seem to already "know it all," but others are dedicated to being "lifelong learners." I am put off by know-it-alls, but I am attracted to lifelong learners. Lifelong learners live a life founded on humility, recognizing that they can learn something new from anyone as long as they pay attention. I learned how to create PowerPoint presentations from my oldest daughter when she was in seventh grade—and at the time they revolutionized my teaching as a university professor. Then, a few years ago, my youngest daughter taught me how to text. I initially thought that texting sounded like one of the stupidest things I had ever heard of—until I tried it. And now I love texting—it is the perfect kind of communication for many situations.

The learning life can revolutionize marriages. After several years of marriage, we can start thinking that we have our spouse all figured out. But no one can ever be "figured out" in this life—not only because every person is a unique mysterious masterpiece, created by a master-designer whose intellect is far beyond ours, but also because even if we were to figure someone out, that person would keep on changing, for life changes us. I am embarrassed to admit that I did not learn my wife's primary "love language" until we had been married for thirty-two years. If married men and women could embrace the marvelous mystery that is their spouse and become determined lifelong learners about him or her, we would see far fewer divorces and far more marriages filled with wonder.

Being a learner is the essence of being a disciple of Jesus. In fact, that is what the word "disciple" means: learner and follower. Many church buildings are full of people who think that they understand the basics of Christianity—and so they stop learning. But most lifetime learners learn something new every time they read the Bible, even passages they have read many times before. Going to church, singing praise to God, praying, taking communion, and listening to the Bible preached are not run-of-the-mill activities that exist only to be fodder for critique during Sunday lunch. Rather, they are expressions of worship, each pregnant with the possibility for us to learn more about a mysterious God whom we can never fully "figure out." Many times, our worship is mediocre precisely because our view of God is mediocre.

Living the learning life turns every person whom you encounter into a potential teacher. A newborn child can teach you about dependence and a homeless person about gratitude, and a person from another culture can show you your own blind spots concerning your culture or your theology. For example, some South Korean Christians have said that American Christians seem to be afraid of persecution and of death—and I am stung to realize how true their evaluation is.

My mentally handicapped younger brother has taught me how to welcome people. My three grandchildren have taught me how to smile and enjoy life. Even people who are bad examples can teach us what *not* to do. If Genesis 1:27 is correct in saying that every person is created *in the image of God*, then we can even learn things *about God* from atheists or agnostics, who still bear some of God's image even in their fallen and unbelieving state.

A friend of mine always reminds young people who are about to set out for the day's assignment on a short-term mission trip that they will be in God's classroom for the next twelve hours. Afterward, he asks them what they learned in God's classroom that day. Indeed, we can learn much even by merely looking at nature if we pay attention. The writer of Proverbs tells us to "go to the ant" to learn perseverance and delayed gratification. Jesus tells us to consider the "lilies of the field" and the "birds of the air" to learn not to worry. A monk named Brother Lawrence learned about God's providential care by looking at a leafless tree in the winter and thinking about the blossoms and fruit that would come in the spring.

When the university where I teach asked me to design an online class, I hesitated. For one thing, I wasn't sure that an online environment could facilitate the kind of learning experiences that are possible in face-to-face classroom instruction. But after being trained in the dynamics and mechanics of designing an online class, I finally took on the challenge—and was pleasantly surprised by the experience. I learned that teaching online has both advantages and disadvantages, just like face-to-face classroom instruction.

Indeed, we who live in the information age have no excuse not to learn new things. I loved the Skype sessions I shared with my youngest daughter a few years ago when she was attending a college six hours away from home. I love Skype and FaceTime sessions with my son and his wife, who live in Hawaii. I also love using Skype to connect with former students of mine who are ministering all around the world. I even got up the courage to use Skype in my university classroom. When members of my "Language and Communication" class shared a Skype session with a church-planting missionary couple in Japan, the experience of learning a foreign language came alive for them. A couple of years ago I got my first smartphone, allowing me to carry the world in my pocket, opening up a world of amazing learning opportunities thanks to services such as Google, Wikipedia, and Dictionary.com.

We also have much to learn much from dead people—those who have gone before us. When I teach intercultural studies, I often remind my students that they are standing on the shoulders of Christians who have lived during the previous 2,000 years. We would be arrogant to go about our twenty-first-century mission work without first learning from them. I read from the works of my historical mentor, E. Stanley Jones, almost every morning, along with my Bible. Jones was born in the late nineteenth century and ministered in India for much of the twentieth century, but his many books continue to teach me daily lessons that are relevant and applicable in my own time.

If you have a teachable heart, you can learn from everyone and everything around you. There is always something new to learn if you are paying attention. Face it: You will never know it all, but you can ask God to help you learn as much as possible during the short time he gives you on this amazing Earth. You and I have no excuse for failing to add to our learning until our final breath. I have a feeling that God is going to ask us someday: "What did you learn in my classroom on Earth?"

LIFE APPLICATION

1. What new thing have you always wanted to learn how to do? What new technologies are you afraid to learn to use? Ask someone to teach you how to use them.
2. What can you learn to do in small increments, starting even today?
3. Every morning, ask God to give you a teachable heart, and ask him to help you pay attention to what he wants to teach you during the day.

CHAPTER 9

THE TRUTHFUL LIFE

Life is too short to fake it

"If you hold to my teaching, you are really my disciples.
Then you will know the truth, and the truth will set you free."
John 8:31–32

"If we walk in the light, as he is in the light, we have fellowship with
one another, and the blood of Jesus, his Son, purifies us from all sin."
1 John 1:7

We are called to live truthful lives in the middle of a culture of lies and deception. News today has given way to spin, manipulation of the facts to put politicians, business leaders, and entertainers in the best possible light. But Christians have been warned not to conform to this world (Rom 12:2).

Many people live their whole lives behind a mask, afraid to show anyone their real self. By doing so, we become skilled at wearing multiple masks, even trading one mask for another to suit the occasion. Our Sunday morning "church mask" might be very different from our "work mask" or our "spouse mask."

The Church should be the safest place on Earth to be our true selves, yet even among members of our church we often play games, pretending that everything is fine: "Oh, I'm just happy in Jesus!" If you are truly happy in Jesus, then great; but if you are down in the dumps or troubled by something, then you should be able to say so openly to your Christian family. Sometimes we are afraid to tell people at church what is really going on in our life, fearing that the information will be passed around "as a prayer request."

A life of pretension can be exhausting and imprisoning. Because our time on Earth is brief, we must waste no time being set free to live the truthful life. Living such a life can be scary, because it means being transparent and vulnerable. Certainly there are risks; but the reward of living a free life, a life with all masks off, is worth it. Honestly living life, with nothing to hide, is incredibly freeing.

1 John 1:7 says that "if we walk in the light," "we have fellowship with one another." Walking in the light can be defined as living a transparent life—having nothing to hide. Living the truthful life is a prelude to and a condition for deep fellowship with others. I once attended a men's breakfast at my church during which a man I'll call Paul, made himself vulnerable, sharing something from his past of which he was very ashamed. He told us how when he was a young man, he had talked his pregnant girlfriend into getting an abortion. When I heard Paul share this story, I immediately felt drawn to him. His vulnerability did not cause me to judge or condemn him. On the contrary, it drew me closer to him. At the same breakfast, a 70-year-old man I'll call Stephen, shared openly about the aggressive sexual temptations with which he had dealt during his life as a truck driver. Every Sunday, I find Stephen and give him a hug. His transparent sharing of his temptations and struggles built a deep bond of fellowship between us. Something about living a truthful life draws people to us. As Christian Anthropologist Paul Hiebert has written, "the price of knowing others is to be known."

I need to warn you that trying to live the truthful life will put you in direct conflict with Satan. Jesus called Satan the "father of lies." Moments before, he said that when Satan speaks, he speaks his native language—lying (John 8:44). Satan is a master deceiver, so we shouldn't be surprised that he particularly likes convincing us that lying is no big deal—just something that everyone does. Satan's lying began in the Garden of Eden, and it continues now. He started by questioning God's word, then he denied God's word and later suspected God's motives. And he does the same things today. Satan is the ultimate master of spin. His goal is to get you separated from God's presence; his ultimate objective is to destroy you. He starts by getting you to believe that a "little white lie" won't hurt anyone. And in so doing, Satan works hard to keep us from being truthful and transparent about ourselves. He knows that the truth will set us free. If he can get us to be deceptive, including by wearing a protective, phony mask, then he can keep us in bondage.

I once struggled to prepare a sermon for our university chapel service, sensing that the Lord wanted me to be very transparent about my personal struggles with temptation and sin. But then Satan began to whisper lies in my ears. He said, "Students and faculty will lose respect for you"; he said, "If you share about the real you, people won't like you." I felt great pressure to put on the "Christian university professor" mask, pretending that I had everything together. But in the end, the Lord gave me courage to be honest. I shared about my long-term struggle with pornography and the brokenness in my life that resulted from my having been emotionally and sexually abused during childhood. And the response to my chapel sermon was absolutely amazing. I discovered that transparency will raise you in the eyes of others, not lower you. People can handle the truth! And because of my willingness to be truthful and transparent, many students have sought me out for counsel. The truthful life is certainly not an easy one, but it is a powerful catalyst for ministry.

Living the truthful life can also have a significant effect on your family, and especially on your children. Proverbs 20:7 says, "The righteous man leads a blameless life; blessed are his children after him." I used to become discouraged when I read the word *blameless* in Scripture; taking it to mean perfection—something I could never attain. But one day I had a new thought: *If I confess,* blaming myself first *for my sin, then others can't blame me——I have already done the blaming!* It was possible after all for Michael Nichols to be a blameless man! Living the truthful life will lead to living a blameless life, because no one will ever be able to dig up dirt on you—you have already shown everyone all the dirt. No one will ever be able to find skeletons in your closet, because you have already opened all your closet doors for everyone to see inside. Living the truthful life will also pull the plug on Satan's accusations, leaving them no more power over you: You will have already accused yourself.

A truthful life is an authentic life, a life of integrity. The Latin root of the word *integrity* means "whole or complete." Having integrity means living a full, complete, and undivided life. When you have integrity, you don't wear masks in different situations; you simply are who you are all the time. To be able to live this kind of life, you must become convinced that God loves you for who you are. He created you to be who you are; you don't have to pretend to be anyone else. The power to live a truthful life will come only when you know in your heart that you have been "fearfully and wonderfully made" (Ps 139:14) and that you are God's "beloved Child" (1 John 3:1).

Your truth and authenticity will show in all areas of your life. You will have authentic emotions, conversations, and convictions. You will begin to become comfortable in your own skin, not trying to hide who you are from anyone. Authentic people become free from self-consciousness. Because they are no longer using their energy to hide the truth of themselves, they are free to focus on others. People who are truthful about themselves will also be truthful about others—not gossiping or spreading rumors.

One of the most sobering passages in the Bible is Revelation 21:8:

But the cowardly, the unbelieving, the vile, the murderers, the sexually immoral, those who practice magic arts, the idolaters *and all liars*—their place will be in the fiery lake of burning sulfur. This is the second death.

When you read this passage, as well as the stories of the lies of Achan in the Old Testament (Joshua 7) and of Ananias and Sapphira in the New Testament (Acts 5), you will realize how important truth is to God.

My daughter Sarah once gave me for Father's Day a list of twenty-eight reasons why she loved me—one for each year of her life. The twenty-fourth particularly encouraged me: "I love watching you struggle so transparently, so humanly, with your flaws. People are drawn to your honest struggle." How glad I am to have been able to bless my daughter by living the truthful life! Make no mistake: There are people in your life who will be blessed by your truthful living. Faking it will help no one.

LIFE APPLICATION

1. When are you most tempted to put on a mask and pretend?
2. Think of someone you know who is truthful and authentic. What do you like about that person's words, actions, and attitudes? How can you begin to follow his or her example to live your own truthful life?
3. What can you do to remind yourself to just be you, not pretending to be someone you aren't?

CHAPTER 10

THE COURAGEOUS LIFE
Life is too short to live in fear

"Have I not commanded you? Be strong and courageous.
Do not be terrified; do not be discouraged, for the LORD
your God will be with you wherever you go."
Joshua 1:9

"There is no fear in love. But perfect love drives out fear."
1 John 4:18

I have spent much of my sixty years living in fear. From an early age, I was afraid of my dad, fearful that he would hit or spank me. I was afraid of girls from grade school all the way through college. I have always been self-conscious, afraid of what people thought about me. I decided to become a Christian out of fear. When I was nine years old, I had nightmares about dying and going to hell. I knew I was a sinner—I had no difficulty believing that I deserved to be condemned to hell and that I needed God to save me. Even after giving my life to God and following him, I often feared that God was waiting to punish me. Imagine how freeing it would have been for me to go through life unafraid!

A visiting speaker from one of Lincoln Christian University's sister colleges, Mark Moore, once spoke to our student body about fear. He told students that the word *fear* showed up more than 500 times in the Bible, and then he explained that God clearly commanded us to fear only two things. He asked the students to name them. They got the first one quickly—we are commanded to fear God—but were stuck on the second one. The second thing, Mark explained, was "nothing." He pointed out the many times when the Bible says, "Fear not!" Scripture clearly teaches us that we are to fear God—and nothing else. Mark asked the students what they would be willing to do for God if he took their fears away. He then challenged the students to write heartfelt prayers concerning their fears. That night, the students used permanent markers to fill dozens of poster boards with honest, gut-wrenching prayers about all the things they feared. Students wrote prayers about many things including: fear of poverty, fear of leaving family, fear of living in a foreign country, fear of speaking in front of people, fear about finding a mate, fear of disappointing family, fear of rejection, and fear of failure.

Naming our fears is helpful; only then can we begin to pray specifically about them. God usually does one of two things with our fears. He can take them completely away—and how awesome when he does! But he doesn't seem often to do that. Usually God gives us courage to face our fears instead. Courage is not the absence of fear, but rather doing something even when we are afraid. If you were to ask a fireman whether he is afraid of entering a burning building—or a soldier whether he is afraid of going into battle—both would probably admit to their fear. But courage is what allows them to go anyway.

Life is too short to always be playing it safe. Most of life's significant events don't happen in the comfort zone. Our society has elevated safety perhaps too much. Of course there is wisdom in basic safety—but if we make safety our highest priority, we run the risk of losing our courage to face our fears. In his book *Just Courage*, Christian human rights activist Gary Haugen asks parents a penetrating question: "Do you want your kids to be safe, or do you want them to be brave?" Some parents have so overemphasized physical safety that they end up endangering their children spiritually.

Gary Haugen, who sees many American Christians as being trapped in a world of suburban monotony and triviality, uses the metaphor of a cul-de-sac to illustrate how Americans endanger their kids spiritually by keeping them "safe at home." The literal meaning of cul-de-sac is "dead-end street." It has been a regular feature of suburban housing developments for many years, designed to alleviate homeowner anxieties about traffic dangers, by eliminating high-speed traffic that would endanger children playing on sidewalks and streets. In the search for a pathway to safety, the cul-de-sac was created. But decades later, studies revealed that cul-de-sacs are actually more dangerous for children. Children are not injured by forward-moving traffic as often as they are by cars that are backing up—which is exactly what people do in cul-de-sacs. Now many cities want to ban cul-de-sac developments because they increase risk to children. Parents who want their kids to be safe, could actually endanger them when they try to remove all risk from their lives. Many "spiritually at-risk" youth in churches, who are constantly exposed to materialism in places such as suburban malls, could be challenged to face their fears by making a difference in an "unsafe" inner-city neighborhood or on the mission field in another country.

Leaving your comfort zone and going to a different place that doesn't seem as safe does take courage. In fact, I covet your prayers—because being an intercultural studies/missions professor, a lot of parents don't like me! The fact is, many of the world's neediest mission fields are the world's least safe places.

One of our greatest fears is the fear of dying. I challenge my missions students to settle the "death question" (*Am I ready and willing to die?*) deep within their hearts before they ever set foot on the mission field. Doing so will be one of the most freeing things they ever do, because settling the question means coming to a place in life where you are at peace with dying. It is not that you *want to die*, nor that you are *trying to die*—but rather that you are okay if you die—ready whenever the Lord decides to take you home.

Over the last several years, I have returned to the DR Congo on several short term ministry trips. Even though I lived in the DR Congo for a decade, going there still requires courage. Before I leave on each trip, I take a personal inventory, sharing my heart with the Lord and asking him for the courage to face my fears, letting him know that I have settled the death question: I am ready. Every time I settle this question in my heart, I experience deep peace that allows me to go anywhere and do anything—without fear.

It is one thing to face our fears about what happens *after death*, but it is another thing to fear the pain that may attend the process of dying. Dr. Wayne Shaw, dean emeritus of Lincoln Christian Seminary, wrote an email message to the faculty in December 2010 after discovering that he had Multiple Myeloma—bone marrow cancer:

None of us knows what you or I will have to go through before seeing Jesus face to face, but we do know that he is with us, and that we were raised with him in our baptism to begin our resurrected life here and now. Therefore, death is the least of the things that can separate us from the love of God in Christ Jesus our Lord.

Similarly, Moishe Rosen, the founder of the organization Jews for Jesus, reflected on life and death after being diagnosed with Prostate cancer that metastasized, went to his spine, and eventually took his life:

A lot is standing on the way that I'll die. And what is standing is my willingness to endure whatever God has for me, which will be the capstone on a testimony of redemption. Nobody likes pain, but there's something with the pain that's bothersome, and that's uncertainty: will I be able to endure it? Will I behave with dignity? What I need is the assurance that the Lord will see me through, and that I can testify to His reality and to His presence as I make the big exit off of life's stage. (*Messianic Times*, May/June 2009)

At certain times in my life, I have sincerely faced the question of my death. Once the question came during a moment of intense pain. Lying on the concrete floor of the bathroom in our house in the DR Congo, thanks to some parasites that were doing major battle with my abdomen, I was in extreme pain, and it wouldn't go away. With my face pressing against the cold concrete, I prayed a very honest prayer: "God, I love my wife and kids, but I am ready to go be with you if this pain won't go away. I am ready to go—take me now, Lord!"

Everyone is afraid of something. Sometimes our fears are rooted in the past, the present, or the future—or perhaps in all three. Yet many of our fears are irrational ones. I have a fear of horses, my wife of snakes, my daughter Sammy of spiders, and my daughter Sarah of bananas (it's kind of a long story!). Perhaps you are afraid of heights, water, airplanes, confined spaces, open spaces, the dark, or speaking in public. You might fear abandonment, failure, meaninglessness, intimacy, change, decision-making, urban areas, or even success. If you can take the time to do a personal inventory, then you will be ready to take the next step: casting your fears upon the Lord (1 Pet 5:7).

My wife Julie told me how scared she was when, as a 20-year-old single girl, she felt called to go to the DR Congo. She was scared to death. After deciding to go, she almost backed out. But as I look back now on our thirty-seven-year marriage, our decade of missionary service in Africa, twenty-five years of serving at Lincoln Christian University, our three children and their spouses, and our three precious grandchildren, I shudder to think that none of that would exist had Julie succumbed to her fear. Had she backed out of going to the DR Congo, we never would have met!

A few years ago, I was inspired by the funeral of a dear older man, Joe, who had been a dedicated Christian his whole life, serving on the mission field in South Korea. After his health deteriorated in 2010, he entered hospice care and was ready to die. The family gathered around him to say their final goodbyes, but Joe ended up living three years longer after removal of his ventilator. As someone said at Joe's funeral, "he wasn't afraid to die, and he also wasn't afraid to live." I want to be like Joe. Life is too short to be afraid to live—or afraid to die.

LIFE APPLICATION

1. What do you fear? Can you name your fear right now? What would you be willing to do for God if he took away your fear or gave you courage to face it?

2. After labeling your fear, write an honest prayer that you can put where you will see it daily. Ask God to either take away your fear or give you courage to face your fear.

3. When you are afraid, use the following short, "breath" prayers, "I will fear no evil, for you are with me"; "Push away the darkness, Jesus"; "Deliver me from the evil one", "Perfect love casts our fear."

CHAPTER 11

THE PEACEFUL LIFE

Life is too short to spend it worrying

"Cast all your anxiety on him because he cares for you."
1 Peter 5:7

*"Do not be anxious about anything, but in everything by prayer
and petition, with thanksgiving, present your requests to God.
And the peace of God, which transcends all understanding, will
guard your hearts and your minds in Christ Jesus."*
Philippians 4:6–7

Worry comes from focusing on what could happen in the future. We serve a God who is timeless: He already knows the future and has it under control. Jesus is the Prince of Peace: He can give us peace in exchange for our anxieties, but only when we give them to him. I once heard a story that illustrates our reluctance to give God our worries: A man was walking down the road with a heavy bag slung over his shoulder when another man driving a horse-drawn wagon pulled alongside and offered him a lift. He accepted the ride, but when he sat on the bench next to the driver, he kept his bag slung over his shoulder. The driver asked, "Why don't you put that burden down in the back of the wagon?" but the man replied, "Oh, it was kind enough of you to give me a ride—you don't have to carry my burden, too." A silly story, but it illustrates how silly we are when we don't let God carry our burden of worries.

There are always plenty of things we could be concerned about, but Jesus doesn't want us to waste our time worrying needlessly. Jesus's classic teaching about worry is found in his Sermon on the Mount:

Therefore I tell you, do not worry about your life, what you will eat or drink; or about your body, what you will wear. Is not life more important than food, and the body more important than clothes? Look at the birds of the air; they do not sow or reap or store away in barns, and yet your heavenly Father feeds them. Are you not much more valuable than they? Who of you by worrying can add a single hour to his life?

And why do you worry about clothes? See how the lilies of the field grow. They do not labor or spin. Yet I tell you that not even Solomon in all his splendor was dressed like one of these. If that is how God clothes the grass of the field, which is here today and tomorrow is thrown into the fire, will he not much more clothe you, O you of little faith? So do not worry, saying, "What shall we eat?" or "What shall we drink?" or "What shall we wear?" For the pagans run after all these things, and your heavenly Father knows that you need them. (Matt 6:25–32)

In this text, Jesus says *Stop worrying, because it is useless!* Worrying won't do anything for you. It can't add any more time to your life, but it sure can steal precious time from your brief life on Earth. Have you ever worried about something you feared would happen and spent a lot of time and emotional energy worrying about it, only for it to never happen? Worry just isn't worth it! When I think about all the time and emotional energy I spent between ages 20 and 24 worrying about whether I would ever find a marriage partner, I wish I had it all back. Worrying about things over which we have no control is foolish—and those things are most things. We live under the grand illusion that we actually have control over things, but we don't. We do, however, have a choice about what to do: We can worry, or we can trust God. Worry is probably the most unproductive thing we humans do. It doesn't help anything or anyone. It doesn't make relationships, finances, or jobs any better. It doesn't make us look any better or feel any better. It doesn't make us more enjoyable to be around. It can't stop something bad from happening or make things any better if it does happen. Worry is absolutely useless!

Worry is also very unhealthful. It can cause headaches, insomnia, chest pains, nervous breakdowns, ulcers, and high blood pressure. You may have heard someone say, "It's not so much what you eat that kills you, but rather *what eats you*." Indeed, worry has reached epidemic proportions in our country. A huge percentage of deaths in our country are caused in part by our worrying lifestyles. Americans consume millions of dollars worth of anti-anxiety pills every year. Worry and anxiety drain us mentally, physically, emotionally, and spiritually. At its core, worry is a spiritual problem: Either we trust God with stuff, or we don't.

In the final verse of Jesus's teaching on worry, he tells us to stop worrying, for worry makes us look like pagans. He said, "The pagans run after all these things, and your heavenly Father knows that you need them." Jesus is saying *Don't you have any faith? Are you an atheist?* The opposite of worry is faith. Jesus is saying *Don't be a pagan; don't live as if I don't exist.* Many churches are full of "practical atheists"—people who call themselves Christians but who live as if God doesn't exist. So should worry be called a sin? Yes, because Jesus *commands us not to worry.* If we go ahead and worry, then we are breaking a command of Jesus—in other words, we are sinning. Because worry is sin, we need to take it seriously and confess it, turning from it with God's help.

Jesus wants us to stop worrying about things and focus on him. Once, when he and his disciples came to a village, a woman named Martha opened her home to him. Her sister, Mary, sat at the Lord's feet listening to what he said, but Martha was distracted by all the preparations that were necessary.

She came to him and asked, "Lord, don't you care that my sister has left me to do the work by myself? Tell her to help me!" "Martha, Martha," Jesus answered, "you are *worried and upset about many things*, but only one thing is needed. Mary has chosen what is better, and it will not be taken away from her" (Luke 10:42).

When I first read this story many years ago, I resonated with Martha. I could see myself being worried about all the necessary preparations for having guests in my house. To remember the point of this story, I personalized Jesus's words to Mary and wrote them on a card above my desk: "Michael, Michael, you are worried and upset about many things, but only one thing is needed. Come and sit at my feet."

In Matthew 6:26, Jesus wants us to learn to trust from the birds: "Look at the birds of the air; they do not sow or reap or store away in barns, and yet your heavenly Father feeds them. Are you not much more valuable than they?" When did you last see a bird worry itself into a nervous breakdown? Most of what happens to us in life is beyond our control, so why do we still struggle to trust God with our life? He is all-knowing and all-powerful—and, best of all, he loves us! I know that some of us struggle because we have an inadequate view of God. I have struggled at times to trust him with my future. At times, I have thought *If I trust God with my future, he may ask me to do something difficult, dangerous, or not in my best interest.* The clear message of this text is that if God loves and cares for birds—and certainly he does—then he *cares much more* for us, for we are much more valuable to him.

Jesus also wants us to learn from flowers. Eugene Petersen's paraphrase can help us understand the lesson Jesus is trying to teach us:

Instead of looking at the fashions, walk out into the fields and look at the wildflowers. They never primp or shop, but have you ever seen color and design quite like it? The ten best-dressed men and women in the country look shabby alongside them. If God gives such attention to the appearance of wildflowers—most of which are never even seen—don't you think he'll attend to you, take pride in you, do his best for you? (Matt 6:28–30)

God is saying that if it is his nature to take care of and dress up the flowers—then it is the same for us. Even the output of the best fashion designers in Europe or New York City—the most expensive clothes, even those of the richest man in history, King Solomon, using the brightest dyes and colors—still cannot match the beauty of flowers! If God is trustworthy with birds and flowers, is he not trustworthy with all the details of our lives?

A college friend of mine, named Gary Coleman, lived in the same dorm as me, and we sat on the bench together our first couple years of college basketball. His two favorite phrases were "Don't sweat the small stuff" and "Small potatoes." Both were his way of saying *Stop worrying. God has got this—he is trustworthy.* Worry does not have to be connected to circumstances in our life. In the same circumstances, one person can be absolutely at peace yet another worried to death. Worry and peace come not from circumstances but from the heart—a heart that trusts God or a heart that doesn't.

The key to stop worrying is focusing on God and his will. When we are passionate about doing his will, our own personal concerns and anxieties begin to shrink. A great love can inspire, intensify, purify, and dominate a person's whole being. Then what if that great love is for God? If you love God with all your heart, soul, mind, and strength, you will stop worrying. Isaiah 26:3 says of God, "You will keep in perfect peace him whose mind is steadfast, because he trusts in you."

Another key to stop worrying is living life one day at a time. Jesus said, "Do not worry about tomorrow, for tomorrow will worry about itself. Each day has enough trouble of its own" (Matt 6:34). There is nothing wrong with planning for the future so long as we don't let it open the door to worrying about the future. I once read about a missionary woman who said, "The thought of the next ten years scares me, but the thought of the next twenty-four hours doesn't." In his grace, God doesn't show us the next ten years of our life. We probably couldn't handle that knowledge without worrying. But through God's grace, we can live life one day at a time without worry.

The best thing to do with worries is to turn them into prayers. The Apostle Paul tells us what to do with the things that make us anxious:

Do not be anxious about anything, but in every situation, by prayer and petition, with thanksgiving, present your requests to God. And the peace of God, which transcends all understanding, will guard your hearts and your minds in Christ Jesus. (Phil 4:6–7)

The best thing to do when anxiety begins to bubble up, when fears begin to grip our heart, or when bad scenarios start to come to mind is to stop at once and admit that we have worries—then turn them into prayers. This has worked for me, and it will work for you. The future may bring big problems, but that isn't where our focus should be. Our focus should be on the one who takes us though our problems one day at a time. Some things will be overwhelming to us, but we don't have to worry—nothing overwhelms God! Life is too short to spend it worrying all the time.

LIFE APPLICATION

1. What robs your life of peace? List all the things that worry you, then offer this list to God, one item at a time.
2. Whenever worries pop up during the day, stop—and turn them into prayers. Create a short prayer about peace for you to say throughout the day.
3. Write the words of Philippians 4:6–7 on a card, then place it where you will see it again and again every day. Write the words of this passage on the tablet of your heart—memorize them.

CHAPTER 12

THE HEALING LIFE

Life is too short not to deal with your brokenness

"The LORD is close to the brokenhearted
and saves those who are crushed in spirit."
Psalm 34:18

"I am the LORD, who heals you."
Exodus 15:26

Everyone is broken in some way, and life is far too short not to deal with it. An honest description of who I am would say, "Mike is a broken man who is being healed by Jesus." Brokenness usually comes from two main sources: We can be broken because someone *sinned against us*, and we can be broken because of the *sins we commit*. Ignoring our brokenness and hoping it just goes away can be tempting. Many times we attempt to bury it and forget about it, but then it returns with a vengeance during a time of stress. A key question then becomes, what we do with our brokenness? I have learned that there are at least five helpful things we can do with it.

First, we must *admit* to it. Jesus said, "Blessed are the poor in spirit, for theirs is the kingdom of heaven" (Matt 5:3). Blessing will not come until we admit that we are broken and in need of God's help. I don't think the Apostle Paul ever forgot his brokenness. He said, "Here is a trustworthy saying that deserves full acceptance: Christ Jesus came into the world to save sinners—of whom I am the worst" (1 Tim 1:15). Note that he said "I *am* the worst," not "I *was* the worst."

Once we have admitted that we have brokenness, we can *cry out* to God. We can cry out for both forgiveness and healing. One of the benefits of crying out to God is that Scripture tells us that "the LORD is close to the brokenhearted" (Ps 34:18). I have often advised students who are in pain because of the brokenness in their lives to go and scream and yell at God in their pain. This especially works well in autumn on our campus bordered on one side by a large cornfield. On occasion, I have recommended that students take a walk into the cornfield, shouting their complaints to God.

God deeply understands our pain, and he is big enough to take any negative emotions we have that need letting out. I believe that we can be angry at God and still be respectful. One need look only as far as the psalms of lament in the Old Testament. David cries out to the Lord, "How long, O LORD? Will you forget me forever? How long will you hide your face from me? How long must I wrestle with my thoughts and every day have sorrow in my heart?" (Ps 13:1–2). Have you ever noticed how many prayers of complaint there are in the Bible from believers such as Job and Jeremiah? Greg Pruett, in a powerful little book called *Extreme Prayer*, points out that "complaining is allowed with one major condition: we must continue to faithfully obey and follow him in spite of our suffering."

The third thing we can do is *share* our brokenness with others so that they can help us carry the burden. We were not meant to do life alone. Paul told the Galatian Christians to "carry each other's burdens," saying that "in this way you will fulfill the law of Christ." I can think of at least three different kinds of Christian relationships that can help us with our brokenness. First is that of a friend who can walk alongside us daily in our pain. Another is that of a mentor or spiritual father or mother who can give us wise counsel and guidance. Such a person is someone who has walked farther down the road than we have and who may have even dealt with some of the same kinds of brokenness as we have. A third relationship is with someone who has received special training in helping broken people—for example, a professional counselor or a pastor.

Many people try and keep their pain to themselves, either out of shame and embarrassment or because they don't want to bother someone else with it. But God has created us as creatures who have a deep need for community. The church is supposed to be a "hospital for sinners" where Christians help each other heal. It is important to see how James connects confession with healing: "Therefore confess your sins to each other and pray for each other so that you may be healed" (Jas 5:16). Admitting our brokenness and asking others to help us carry the burden of brokenness is the pathway to healing.

The fourth thing we need to do is *believe that our healing from God will eventually come*. Indeed, it could come immediately. God has the power to heal our brokenness instantaneously, though he seems to do so relatively rarely. More often, God heals us over time, during our life on Earth. And, of course, sometimes God waits to heal us in heaven. The Apostle Paul pleaded with God to remove his thorn in the flesh three different times (2 Cor 12:7–9). But God's answer was no: "My grace is sufficient for you, for my power is made perfect in weakness." We must believe that God will eventually heal us of all the brokenness in our lives. He may do it now, sometime later during our life on Earth, or in heaven, after we die.

One of the reasons why God may delay our "total healing" is because he wants to use our brokenness to grow our character. James tells us to "consider it pure joy" when we "face trials of many kinds," because God uses these trials to develop perseverance in our lives, helping us mature (Jas 1:2). Another reason why God may delay our total healing is because he wants to use us in our broken state to bring comfort to others.

God never wastes a broken area of our life; he wants to turn these areas into ministry opportunities. Our greatest ministry often comes from the most painful and broken areas of our lives. The Apostle Paul encouraged the Corinthian Christians to praise God for his compassion and comfort toward us. And then Paul told them that one of the main reasons why God comforts us in all our troubles is "so that we can comfort those in any trouble with the comfort we ourselves have received from God" (2 Cor 1:4).

Growing up with an abusive father has been one of my deepest areas of wounding and brokenness. By God's grace, it has also become one of the greatest, most influential areas of ministry in my life. Because of my brokenness in this area, I have a deep empathy for anyone who doesn't have a loving father. I also have personal knowledge of what the fatherless really want and need from a father. God has not only been healing my "father wound," but he has also made it into a powerful ministry to others who bear the same kind of wounds.

Life is too short not to deal with our brokenness. My oldest daughter is a licensed professional counselor, and she tells me that one of her favorite counseling questions is "What are you going to do with your pain?" We may be sitting on the most powerful and effective ministry of our life simply because we don't want to open the door to share a secret or face the pain. The God of *all comfort* is waiting, wanting to comfort you so that you can become a comfort to others. Life is too short to miss out on this ministry opportunity.

LIFE APPLICATION

1. What are the most painful and broken areas of your life? Can you name things that come from sin you have committed and things that come from your having been sinned against?

2. Do you have Christian people in your life from each of the three different areas (friend, mentor or spiritual parent, counselor or

pastor)? Are you willing to begin to pray and search for such people to help you?

3. Have you been able to think of how to use the brokenness and pain in your life as a pathway to ministry? Would you be willing to brainstorm with someone about ministry ideas?

CHAPTER 13

THE CONTENTED LIFE

Life is too short to be discontented

*"I know what it is to be in need, and I know what it is to have plenty. I
have learned the secret of being content in any and every situation."*
Philippians 4:12

*"But godliness with contentment is great gain. For we brought
nothing into the world, and we can take nothing out of it. But
if we have food and clothing, we will be content with that."*
1 Timothy 6:6–8

We live in a very discontented society, surrounded by
discontented people. The media constantly tell us not to be
content with what we have. We are constantly told that we
need a newer car, a more powerful computer, a smarter phone, and cooler
clothes. We never seem to have enough of anything. But then we fill our lives
with so many possessions we don't even use that we have to rent storage units
just to hold all our stuff. Living the contented life means being satisfied with

what you have, feeling that you have enough. Contented people are at peace with their circumstances and their possessions. Thinking about death and the brevity of life can help give us contentment. Why would you ever want to trust in things? You can't take even one with you beyond the grave.

You've seen the bumper stickers: "He who dies with the most toys wins." More truthful ones read, "He who dies with the most toys—still dies" or "He who dies with the most toys—leaves them all here." An old Spanish proverb says, "There are no pockets in a burial shroud." And you never see a U-Haul trailer hooked to a hearse.

When we travel by plane, we wonder how much baggage we are allowed, but when it comes to death, we know the answer already: No carry-ons allowed! After John D. Rockefeller's death, a journalist bent on determining how much Rockefeller had been worth financially at the time of his death asked one of Rockefeller's top aides, "How much money did Rockefeller leave behind?" The aide responded, "All of it."

How easily we fall into the trap of thinking that things can bring us happiness and contentment. It is easy to think *if I just had enough things* ... The Bible uses the word *envy* to describe the attitude of a discontented person. Proverbs 14:30 says, "A heart at peace gives life to the body, but envy rots the bones." If you aren't satisfied with what you have, you will never be satisfied with what you want. The Bible also has a great deal to say about greed. A greedy person is never contented, always wanting more. In his book, *Celebration of Discipline*, Richard Foster writes about American levels of discontentment and greed crossing the line into insanity: "We buy things we do not need to impress people we do not like."

Juliet Schor, in *The Overspent American*, talks about our desire to "keep up with the Joneses." She says that the Joneses are no longer the people who live next door—because we hardly know our neighbors any more. Rather, the "reference groups" that we form at work and play are the groups with which we compare ourselves, the groups whose members tell us what we should acquire if we are to be "successful." She says that the desire for designer clothes and expensive shoes begins in preschool. She reports having surveyed a telecommunication corporation that has 85,000 employees. She found that each hour of weekly television viewing reduced annual savings by $208. Those who were surveyed reported that it wasn't really the commercials— but rather the lifestyles portrayed in the programs—that most affected their attitudes toward spending.

The world tries to seduce us from every television, radio, and billboard and in every computer popup. Its message is clear: *Don't be content! You must have more, better, faster, and newer.* The world sells discontentment.

One of the greatest skills you can develop in this culture of discontent is talking back to or yelling back at commercials and advertisements. You can make it a habit to yell, "I have enough! I don't need that!" or "I can be happy without that!" One of the greatest negative consequences of living in a culture of discontent is that everyone gets into debt. Much of our debt comes from our discontentment. Preacher David Stone's acronym for the word *debt* might help: He says it should stand for, "Don't Even Buy That!" Think of how many times people go into debt thinking *if I just had this one thing, then my life would be better.*

Several years ago in Dallas, Texas, I heard Denny Slaughter preach about contentment. Denny had always wanted to buy a nice little Honda self-propelled push mower to mow his yard. He thought *if I just had one of those mowers, mowing the yard would be enjoyable. I would be so contented.* So he went out and bought one, and he did really enjoy it—until a friend warned him one day that his model of mower was so popular in the city that it was often stolen right out of people's yards. Suddenly Denny's contentment vanished. He couldn't take a break from mowing to drink a glass of iced tea without worrying that someone would steal his mower. He began to worry about whether he had left the garage door up when he was away. His life of contentment became a life of worry. Things can do that to you. The very things we think will bring us contentment can bring us discontent.

A great question to ask ourselves is whether we possess our possessions—or are possessed by them. Corrie Ten Boom, who survived a Nazi concentration camp, talks about holding onto things loosely. She says that one reason why she does so is because when she holds to a thing too tightly, she gets hurt when the Lord has to pry her fingers off it. We don't need to hold tightly to things, because we know that the only thing we get to take to heaven is ourselves. People who live the contented life know that having things does not give you what the Bible calls "the life that is truly life," the kind of life that Paul wanted Timothy to live and to teach others how to live:

Command those who are rich in this present world not to be arrogant nor to put their hope in wealth, which is so uncertain, but to put their hope in God, who richly provides us with everything for our enjoyment. Command them to do good, to be rich in good deeds, and to be generous and willing to share. In this way they will lay up treasure for themselves as a firm foundation for the coming age, so that they may *take hold of the life that is truly life.* (1 Tim 6:17–19)

The key to living a contented life is to trust that God will take care of you. How ironic that the words "In God We Trust" are stamped on U.S. coins. A more truthful motto would be "In Money We Trust." Jesus tells us we can't serve him and money at the same time. They are rival masters (Matt 5:24). Jesus also tells us to store up our treasures in heaven, because earthly treasures will rot, rust, or be stolen (Matt 5:19–21). The writer of Hebrews says,

Keep your lives free from the love of money and be content with what you have, because God has said, "Never will I leave you; never will I forsake you." So we say with confidence, "The Lord is my helper; I will not be afraid. What can man do to me?" (Heb 13:5–6)

We must learn to trust in God, because he never changes. He is always there. God doesn't lose value thanks to inflation. God is not subject to downturns in the market. God is not affected by tornadoes, hurricanes, tsunami, or earthquakes. God is absolutely trustworthy.

Paul knew that the secret of contentment is to trust in the Lord. After saying that he had learned to be content whatever the circumstances, he revealed the secret: "I can do everything through him who gives me strength" (Phil 4:13). Jesus taught that trusting our heavenly Father would solve our worries about being provided for (Matt 6:25–27). Contented people don't worry about tomorrow, because they trust God, who is already there.

A few years ago, one of my friends attended a MOPS (Mothers of Pre-Schoolers) conference in Chicago, Illinois, in which a speaker described her meeting with a woman named Ella, who was from Africa. Ella had next to nothing, but she was full of contentment and joy. When asked to share her secret of contentment, Ella described five habits she had in her life. The speaker called them "Ella's Five Holy Habits of Contentment":

- Never complain, even about the weather.
- Never picture yourself somewhere else.
- Never compare yourself with another.
- Never wish this or that had been different.
- Never dwell on tomorrow: It is God's.

This list of habits is simple, yet profound. Some of the most contented people I know live in the DR Congo. I love spending time with my Congolese friend Lwahira. He lives in a house made of bamboo and mud, and his kids sleep on mats on the dirt floor—but he is one of the most contented men I know.

Another secret to contentment is realizing that you don't actually own your stuff: You are just managing it for God. In America, we grow up with a strong sense of personal ownership of our possessions. If you grew up with siblings, you will remember yelling at your brother or sister, "That is *mine!*" I learned a lesson about ownership while serving as a missionary in the DR Congo. My wife and I saved our money for a long time to buy a new vehicle. We asked supporters to give toward our vehicle project and eventually used some of our personal retirement funds to purchase an almost new four-wheel-drive pickup truck. Because we bought the truck in a neighboring country, we had to wait several days on the paperwork before we could bring it home. The day the truck was finally released and brought to our home, I stood outside, shouting in Swahili, "*gari yangu imefika!*"—"*my* truck has arrived!" My Congolese friends were shouting the same phrase, with one word different: "*gari yetu imefika!*"—"*our* truck has arrived!" At first I thought *wait a minute—this is* my *truck, not yours!* It was a lesson about living in a collectivistic society, in which possessions were owned by the group, rather than an individualistic society such as America. But then the Lord taught me a greater lesson. He reminded me that all the money used to purchase the truck—whether received as gifts, earned as salary, or taken from retirement funds—actually came from him; it wasn't *our money* in the first place. Then the Lord reminded me that the truck was to be used for his kingdom work in the DR Congo: He was the owner; I was the manager.

The world wants to make us into greedy consumers, but God wants to make us into faithful stewards who manage his things well. As long as we remember who owns everything, we can live a contented life. Life is too short to be discontented.

LIFE APPLICATION

1. Do you have clutter in your life? Simplify your life by getting rid of possessions you don't need or use. Spend time at the local landfill reflecting on how many things in life are temporary.

2. Are you possessed by your possessions? How can you begin to hold onto them with open hands? Carry around a little card labeled "nuff," reminding you that you always have—wait for it—a *nuff!*

3. Do you play the comparison game? Do you play the "when … then" game (*when* I have this, *then* I will be content)? Choose some phrases

you can say when you see something someone else has or when you see an advertisement trying to sell you something. For example: "I don't need that to be happy!"

CHAPTER 14

THE SUFFERING LIFE

Life is too short not to carry your cross

"If anyone would come after me, he must deny himself and take up his cross and follow me."
Matthew 16:24

"It is easier to wear a cross than to bear one."
Mike Baker

T he cross is often mysteriously absent in the theology taught in many American churches. It might show up in reference to Jesus's death on the cross, but it is often missing as a sign of discipleship. Many American Christians simply don't see suffering as part of the normal Christian life. In an interview several years ago, Elizabeth Elliot—a former missionary to Ecuador whose husband, Jim, had been killed by the Waodani more than fifty years ago—was asked what she thought was missing in evangelical churches in America. Without hesitation she said,

Sacrifice and commitment are overlooked themes in the church today. They were overlooked themes when Jesus first articulated them. There were not very many people who wanted to follow him after he made it perfectly clear that if you want to be his disciple you must give up your right to yourself. That has to be the hardest thing God asks of us. And he puts it right up front. No *ifs*, *ands*, or *but*s.

In today's world, we are constantly bombarded with messages telling us to focus on ourselves: "If it feels good, do it"; "It's your life—do what you want." To speak about a daily cross of suffering in such a context doesn't seem to fit. How tempted we can be to shape Christianity into something a little less demanding, a little more comfortable. But even so, the call to Christian discipleship is a call for nothing less than death to self and sacrificial service of Christ. That often means suffering. But sometimes we have misinterpreted Jesus's call to take up our cross and follow him. We often use the phrase *bearing my cross* to mean putting up with something. I've been a Chicago Cubs baseball fan all my life, so when someone mentions the long dearth of World Series appearances for the Cubs (up until 2016!), I'm tempted to say, "Oh, that's just the cross I have to bear." People use the phrase for everything from wearing glasses to being short or having acne. But that's not what Jesus had in mind. Crosses were not inconvenient burdens to be carried; they were cruel instruments of death. In 1937, Dietrich Bonhoeffer wrote a sentence that became one of the most famous theological sentences of the twentieth century: "When Christ calls a man, he bids him *come and die.*" It was a statement that Bonhoeffer backed up with his own blood, shed at the hands of a Nazi executioner.

Once one of my teaching colleagues, Mike Baker, was looking through his mail. He had just received a catalogue featuring religious jewelry. As he flipped through the catalogue, he started making fun of all the different kinds of crosses, asking me, "Hey, Mike—would you like a sterling silver cross, a gold-plated one, or maybe one made of pearl?" Then he said something so profound that I wrote it down. Mike said, "It's easier to wear a cross *than to bear a cross.*" Maybe part of our problem with crosses is that they seem more like shiny jewelry than the object of scandal that they were during the first century. In an age when we are addicted to comfort, we need to reclaim the scandal of the cross. The cross was a symbol of torture and death, not a piece of jewelry. Jesus's call to "take up our cross" was a call to sacrifice and suffering, not a call to comfort. Even so, I struggle with this, for like so many, I find myself insulated from much of the world's pain and suffering.

If we can reconnect with the original meaning of the cross, we might be able to reconnect with suffering as a normal part of following Jesus. The cross is a religious symbol now, but in the first century it was only a scandal—a way of executing the worst criminals. To reclaim the shock value of the cross, one author recommended using other words for capital punishment (for example, *hangman's noose, firing squad,* or *electric chair*) as a replacement for the word *cross* in some of our favorite hymns, such as *The Old Rugged Cross* or *When I Survey the Wondrous Cross.* We have become too comfortable with the cross.

A Roman crucifixion was not a pretty picture. The Romans created a death that was as cruel, degrading, and painful as possible, as described in detail by Martin Hengel in his book *Crucifixion.* First the victim was stripped naked and scourged—a brutal beating during which men often died. But part of the suffering of the cross was humiliation. The victim was nailed to the crossbeam and lifted up for public display. As the hours passed, the body suffered from blood loss, exposure, and traumatic shock. Savage thirst and pain racked the victim, his or her body weight thrown forward against the pectoral muscles, making breathing increasingly difficult. Finally, when exhaustion made the effort of breathing impossible, the crucified person suffocated. Roman statesmen Cicero called crucifixion "the supreme capital penalty, the most painful, dreadful, and ugly." Such a hideous death was reserved for the worst of slaves and foreigners—not for Roman citizens. Jesus's first disciples had a problem accepting the scandal of the cross—and especially that their leader would die in such a cruel way. The Apostle Paul wrote

But we preach Christ crucified: a stumbling block to Jews and foolishness to Gentiles, but to those whom God has called, both Jews and Greeks, Christ the power of God and the wisdom of God. (1 Cor 1:23–24)

A. W. Tozer argued that we still like to avoid the scandal of the cross today:

The cross of popular evangelicalism is not the cross of the New Testament. It is, rather, a new bright ornament upon the bosom of a self-assured and carnal Christianity. The old cross slew men, the new cross entertains them. The old cross condemned; the new cross amuses. The old cross destroyed confidence in the flesh; the new cross encourages it.

There are, of course, many different kinds of suffering in life. Some suffering comes as a direct consequence of our own sinful choices or other people's sinful choices. Other suffering comes directly from Satan and his demons or indirectly, through people used as Satan's pawns. Still other suffering is a result of God's discipline, as he continues to build into us the character of Christ. Suffering is made even more difficult when we don't know its source or can't explain it. I do not fully understand the suffering of my former student Steve Szoke—a young man with such a heart for evangelism. I don't understand why my friend Phil Rogers had to leave the mission field suffering from a debilitating disease. He was serving as a Christian missionary in a Muslim-majority country in Africa, and there aren't many people standing in line for that job. Why did they have to suffer? I don't know, but I do know that suffering is a normal part of being a disciple of Jesus.

The Bible clearly tells us that suffering is part of the normal life of discipleship. Jesus told his disciples not to be surprised by suffering; rather, he told them straight out that if the world persecuted him, then it would persecute them, too (John 15:18–21). Peter told believers not to be surprised by painful trials of suffering as if something strange were happening (1 Pet 4:12–13); rather, he told them to rejoice at being given the chance to participate in the sufferings of Christ. Paul told Timothy that "everyone who wants to live a godly life in Christ Jesus will be persecuted" (2 Tim 3:12).

Suffering is a topic that many American Christians simply want to ignore. Some churches resort to teaching half of the gospel, focusing on the blessings of God but not on his call to radical discipleship that includes suffering. This heresy is known by many names, such as "health and wealth" teaching or the "prosperity gospel." Even evangelistic methods can easily be hijacked by this heresy. The "Four Spiritual Laws" written by Campus Crusade founder Bill Bright begin with the affirmation "God loves you and offers a wonderful plan for your life." I agree, but many Americans interpret "wonderful plan" to mean a life without suffering.

The Old Testament prophet Isaiah predicted that the promised Messiah would be "familiar with suffering" (Isa 53:3). Jesus was certainly familiar with suffering, both in his death and in his earthly life. He experienced the suffering of family rejection, betrayal by a friend, and homelessness. During crucifixion, he suffered three specific kinds of abuse. Besides the obvious physical abuse of scourging and nailing to a cross, he suffered the verbal and emotional abuse of being mocked, cursed at, and spat upon. But he suffered another form of abuse as well—sexual abuse. Jesus was almost certainly crucified naked, which was part of the public humiliation of crucifixion. Having your clothes ripped off to expose your nakedness in public definitely qualifies as a form of sexual abuse. No wonder the writer of Hebrews says that Jesus is a high priest who can sympathize with our weaknesses (Heb 4:15). Our theology of suffering must include Jesus's understanding of the suffering we go through in life.

We must also understand that Jesus's suffering was entirely voluntary. When I was a college student, I watched a reenactment of the crucifixion at a church camp in Missouri one summer. I thought the campers did a pretty fair job of being realistic when I heard the sounds of hammers hitting nails, saw ketchup being used for blood, and saw people spitting at Jesus. But when those standing by the cross mocked Jesus, shouting, "If you are the Son of God, come down from there!" I was shocked. The person playing Jesus got down off the cross—and walked away over the hill. As everyone sat in stunned silence, a person got up and said, "You know, Jesus could have done that. The nails didn't hold him on the cross—his love did." Jesus bore his cross for us. Life is too short not to carry ours.

LIFE APPLICATION

1. Do you own any cross jewelry? How can you remind yourself of the scandal of the cross when wearing it?
2. How can you use the symbol of the cross as a symbol of daily discipleship, not just a symbol of your salvation?
3. How can you remind yourself that suffering is a normal part of the Christian life? What Scripture can you memorize or put on a card where you will see it often?

CHAPTER 15

THE JOYFUL LIFE

Life is too short not to enjoy the journey along the way

"Rejoice in the Lord always. I will say it again: Rejoice!"
Philippians 4:4

"A cheerful heart is good medicine."
Proverbs 17:22

Celebration is a major theme in the Bible. Yet I have heard a preacher describe sour-faced Christians who look as if they have been "baptized in vinegar and weaned on a pickle." Life can be serious—and we need to be serious about serious things—but life can also be very funny. We need to learn to lighten up and laugh. I never used to have a picture in my mind of Jesus smiling or laughing until I saw a painting of him laughing while he played with children. The painting was a depiction of the scene from Mark 10 when Jesus told his disciples to let the little children come to him so that he could bless them. I now have a print of that painting hanging on my office wall to remind me of Jesus's lighter side. How can anyone be around little kids for long without laughing? Sometimes we need to remind ourselves that God himself created smiles and laughter, as well as the ability to have a sense of humor.

I will never forget the day when a little girl named Lyndi made me laugh until it hurt. And it happened on one of the most sobering, painful and stressful days of my life. In fall 1991, all the missionaries in eastern DR Congo evacuated the country to escape political unrest. The country was coming apart at the seams. Rioting, looting, killing, and raping had erupted in the capital city of Kinshasa and were spreading across the country to other major cities. Being the field coordinator for our group of missionaries, I had to stay an extra day in the country to wait for our mission pilot to fly the rest of our missionaries into the city from their jungle stations. I was standing beside a small van that held my wife and two young children, getting ready to say goodbye to them. The van was part of a long line of vehicles at the border, carrying missionaries and Peace Corps volunteers who were evacuating the country. I hoped to join my family the next day in Bujumbura, Burundi, but there was no telling what would happen in this self-destructing country. As I stood there, worried—in fact, scared to death—I heard laughter coming from a vehicle behind us. I went back to investigate, thinking *who in the world is laughing on a day like today?* When I found Jay Beeman, a missionary colleague, doubled over in laughter, I asked him, somewhat gruffly, "What in the world is so funny?" He took a moment to compose himself, then told me what his little girl Lyndi had just told him: "Daddy, I am so happy today. God has finally answered my prayer! I have been asking him for a chance to go to Bujumbura with all my missionary friends at the same time, and today he has answered my prayer!" And right then I started laughing, too. God had given me the gift of laughter through the words of a child on the day when I needed it most.

I admit to being overly serious much of the time. I spend a lot of time thinking about serious things, such as reaching the unreached with the gospel and fighting injustice in the world. But I am trying to learn not to take myself so seriously. I try to remind myself that there are serious things in the world, but *I am not one of them.* So when a friend told me that he had forgotten how to have fun, his comment struck a deep chord in me. I thought *I, too, have forgotten.* So I decided to write a note to myself: "Remember how to have fun!" I put it on the opening page of my daily agenda so that I see it every day. Sometimes just seeing that reminder causes me to change my attitude and lighten up. I once heard a speaker describe how he put a small silly toy in his front pants pocket so that whenever he waxed eloquent before a large crowd and was tempted to take himself too seriously, he could put his hand in his pocket—and smile.

One of the great things about living the joyful life is that joy is deeper than happiness. Happiness is connected to circumstances, coming from "what happens." The world tries to use the temporary pleasures of sin to bring a "happiness high" through things such as getting drunk or engaging in illicit sex. The Bible admits that sin can bring pleasure, but such pleasure doesn't last. It is a temporary happiness (Heb 11:25). However, a person can experience deep, long-lasting biblical joy even in the middle of suffering and difficulty. The Apostle Paul uses forms of the word *joy* fourteen times in Philippians, a letter he penned while in prison—no happy circumstance that. In Acts 16, we read about how Paul and Silas sang joyful hymns to God at midnight—in stocks in prison.

Part of living the joyful life is remembering that God is above all circumstances. The prophet Nehemiah said, "The joy of the LORD is your strength" (Neh 8:10). And so I love Henri Nouwen's definition of joy: He says that joy is knowing that you are unconditionally loved by God and that nothing can take his love away. We can obey Paul's command in Scripture, to rejoice at any time, when we use such a definition. In a sense, we can *choose joy* by choosing to focus on the truth of God's love for us. God gives us the power to choose our mood and attitudes. We can choose joy if we want to. As Abraham Lincoln said, "most people are about as happy as they decide to be."

The Bible is full of joy and celebration. The Old Testament contains lots and lots of parties—just think of all the feasts the Lord wanted Israel to enjoy. If you have ever been to a Jewish celebration, you've experienced celebratory singing, dancing, and shouting. The New Testament shows Jesus performing his first miracle at a wedding party, and his partying didn't stop there: Other times, he was questioned by the Jewish leaders about all his "eating and drinking with sinners." Psalm 30:11 says that God can turn our "wailing into dancing." Laughter is truly one of life's best medicines for what ails us. The book of Proverbs contains several verses that relate to joy. Proverbs 17:22 says, "A cheerful heart is good medicine," and Proverbs 15:15 says, "The cheerful heart has a continual feast." I love connecting two verses in Proverbs 15 in particular. Verse 13 says, "A happy heart makes the face cheerful," and verse 30 says, "A joyful look brings joy to the heart." If we focus on the joy in our heart, it will show up on our face—and if people look at the joyful smile on our face, it will create joy in them. Joy flows both ways; joy creates more joy. The description of heaven in Revelation 21 talks about a place with no "mourning, crying, or pain." There will be a lot of laughter and joy in heaven.

My nickname for my youngest daughter is PJ, which stands for "pride and joy." Ever since Sammy was a little girl, I have asked her at bedtime, "What is your job in life?" And she answers, "To give people joy." Sammy grew into the meaning of her nickname and has brought joy into the lives of countless people. A few years ago, Sammy bought me a book I enjoyed—*Love Does*, by Bob Goff. Knowing that I had been reading many serious books for my Ph.D. program, she thought I needed a little whimsy in my life. Indeed, *whimsy* is one of Bob Goff's favorite words. Giving other people joy is the job of every Christian. Joy is contagious. If we are joyful people, our joy will produce more joy in others.

A couple of summers ago, I tried to do some things just for fun. I took my wife to see the latest X-Men movie. We went to Peoria to watch the biggest July 4 fireworks display in Illinois. I attended a minor-league baseball game and borrowed my friend's red Corvette convertible to take my wife out for a drive and a picnic lunch. We all need to do things that make us laugh, for laughter is the music of the soul. We also must take time to play, for play is the secret of perpetual youth. I have found that interacting with children and youth can teach me how to play again. Children exhibit God's creative gift of fantasy and imagination. Playing on the floor with my grandkids, pretending to be with the princess at the king's ball or racing against Lightning McQueen in the Piston Cup, is joyful therapy for me. So is playful teasing in the cafeteria with students who are in their twenties. Similarly, I have found joy in joking together with people in their seventies and eighties who attend my church.

Have you ever been around someone who seems to always enjoy himself or herself, no matter where he or she is? That is the kind of person I want to hang out with, and that is the kind of person I want to be. We are supposed to live the joyful life during our few days here on Earth as we anticipate the eternal, joy-filled party waiting for us in heaven. Life is too short to miss out on the party.

LIFE APPLICATION

1. When was the last time you had a good belly laugh? When was the last time you laughed with your spouse, kids, or grandkids? What things make you laugh? Make a point of scheduling time to play with some small children.

2. Do you struggle with depression? What simple reminder can you put in your life to remind you that you are unconditionally loved? Who do you know who needs joy in his or her life? To whom can you bring joy this week through an intentional act of kindness?

3. Do you take yourself too seriously? Create a daily reminder that says, "Remember how to have fun!" What can you can carry in your pocket to make you laugh? How can you use the creative imagination that God has given you to bring joy to yourself and others?

CHAPTER 16

THE GRATEFUL LIFE

Life is too short not to stop and count your blessings

*"Give thanks in all circumstances, for
this is God's will for you in Christ Jesus."*
1 Thessalonians 5:18

*"The discipline of gratitude is the explicit effort to
acknowledge that all I am and have is given to me as
a gift of love, a gift to be celebrated with joy."*
Henri Nouwen

W hen I lived in the DR Congo, my Congolese brothers and sisters taught me the importance of gratefulness by how they prayed every morning. In the Swahili language, they prayed, "*Asante Mungu sababu niliamuka,*" which means, "Thank you, God, that I woke up." Sometimes they added another sentence: "*Usiku jana nililala kama wafu, halafu leo asubui nilifufuka tena!*" which means "Last night, I went to sleep like a dead person, and this morning I raised again!" The first time I heard this prayer, it stopped me in my tracks and made me ask myself *when was the last time I woke up and thanked God that I woke up?* My first thoughts were usually something like *that cursed alarm clock!* or *where's the coffee?* But after training myself in the daily discipline of gratitude, my first thoughts on waking most mornings are the short prayer *thank you, God, that I woke up!*

We must constantly remind ourselves that our life on Earth, no matter how short or long, is a gift from God. What we do with his gift shows whether we are grateful to God, the gift-giver. In Felice Cohen's *What Papa Told Me*, a book of reflections written by the daughter of a holocaust survivor, I learned how having been a Nazi prisoner made Felice's father truly appreciate simple things after his ordeal ended. He came to appreciate things such as fresh air and the abilities to walk, go to the bathroom, or eat a piece of meat. Often we fail to realize how important something special is until it is gone. For example, on December 20, 2012, a blizzard knocked out the power to my family's home from 4 p.m. to 10 p.m. When the power went off, we couldn't flush the toilets (an electric pump supplies us with well water), wash our hands, or turn on a light. Think how many things we all do each day without thinking about how special they are: walking, talking, hearing, breathing, eating, etc. Death can be like a huge megaphone calling us to appreciate everything—to be thankful for all of life!

So how can we cultivate a grateful life? A couple years ago, I was challenged by a book I was reading to keep a daily gratitude journal. The challenge was simple: Think of three good things that happened today, and record them in your journal. How simple—yet powerful! My attitude shifts immediately when I reflect on three things for which I am thankful. Most days, the three things spring to my mind and begin multiplying, but on some days, thinking of anything can be a little harder. Even on my worst days, however, I eventually find three reasons for gratitude.

I want to learn to be grateful for all the Lord has given me. I don't want to take God or anything he has given me—which is *everything!*—for granted. Brennan Manning says that people who have difficulty trusting especially need to learn gratitude; he calls it leading a *doxological life*, which is to say a life of continual worship. I love reminding my freshman students that if they graduate in four years having earned a bachelor's degree, they will become part of the top 10 percent of the world's most educated "elite." I then ask them if they are grateful for the privilege of attending college. I also love to remind those of my students who were born in the United States that they had absolutely nothing to do with where they were born. I ask them whether they have ever stopped to be thankful that they were born in one of the richest countries the world has ever known.

When I look back on the sixty-one years of my life, I am surprised at how the Lord has blessed me. I have a wonderful wife and amazing kids—who have given me amazing grandkids. I have not gone without food, water, or shelter. I have owned houses, cars, and many possessions. I have been given a wonderful education, including a Ph.D. The ordinary boy who grew up in the small towns of central Illinois has had the privilege of visiting more than twenty-five countries and has been given the opportunity to learn two languages in addition to his mother tongue. Moreover, I have been given opportunities to preach, teach, and publish. I have so much for which to be thankful!

Being grateful can help us in many ways. For one thing, it reminds us of our true wealth. I have always loved the movie *It's a Wonderful Life*, and particularly the Angel Clarence's inscription in the book he gave George Bailey: "No man is a failure who has friends." I'll never forget the day when I learned how wealthy I was. A few years ago, during one of my doctoral class trips to Trinity International University in Deerfield, Illinois, I was riding in a shuttle van between the campus and the train station. Because I was the only one in the van that day, the driver asked whether I wanted to take a short detour to pass by Michael Jordan's house. Because Michael has always been one of my basketball heroes, I jumped at the chance. We were able only to drive up to the iron gate in front of his house; we looked at the number 23 welded to it. I saw the guardhouse, and I saw lift trucks putting up Christmas lights on the trees lining Michael's drive. As I reflected for a moment on the vast wealth of Michael Jordan, I was surprised at the thought that came into my mind: *You, Mike, are wealthier than Michael Jordan*. Michael had recently gone through a failed marriage; moreover, as far as I knew, he was not a believer. When I thought of the value of my solid marriage to Julie as well as all the other blessings I had in Christ, the comparison wasn't even close—I was much wealthier than Michael. Focusing on death reminds us that we can take no possessions with us when we die. James Dobson recorded the prayer his father prayed the last time Jim saw him: "Thank you, God, for what we have, which we know we cannot keep..."

When I travel, I am reminded of how grateful I am for my wife and family. Absence can truly make the heart grow fonder, serving as a stark reminder of who and what is most important. How quick we are to take for granted those whom we love! We forget how valuable people are to us until we don't have them close to us. Because of how quickly we forget our blessings, we must train ourselves in the discipline of stopping to say *thank you*. At Lincoln Christian University, where I teach, I lead a weekly small group of young men whom I decided to train in the discipline of gratitude. Every week, I ask each young man to share not only a prayer request, but also something specific for which he is thankful. Together, we are building an environment and culture of thankfulness by cultivating gratefulness as a regular habit. Someone once challenged me to look at everything as if seeing it *for the first time*—or *the last time*. The first will produce an attitude of wonder, the latter an attitude of gratitude. And how good it is to walk through every day we have on Earth in wonder and gratitude!

LIFE APPLICATION

1. Who are you often tempted to take for granted?
2. Which of your abilities or possessions are you tempted to take for granted?

3. Stop and write down three things for which you are thankful. Keep doing so every day, beginning today—either as soon as you wake up, reflecting on the day before, or before you go to sleep, reflecting on the day that has just passed. If you want, use a notebook or journal to do so.

CHAPTER 17

THE NOURISHED LIFE

Life is too short to be spiritually malnourished

*"Man does not live on bread alone, but on every
word that comes from the mouth of God."*
Matthew 4:4

*"Blessed is the man who does not walk in the counsel of the wicked ...
who's delight is in the law of the LORD and on his law he meditates day
and night. He is like a tree planted by streams of water, which yields its
fruit in season and whose leaf does not wither. Whatever he does prospers."*
Psalm 1:1–3

M any people go to church each week and snack on the word of God by listening to a sermon—then go home and put their Bible on a shelf until the next Sunday rolls around. This behavior is why there are so many weak, spiritually malnourished Christians walking around today. If you eat once a week, you will become sick—perhaps even die. Part of the problem is that many Christians have not been taught how to feed themselves; they are comfortable letting the minister or Sunday school teacher spoon feed them. But eventually, infants must learn to feed themselves. And if baby Christians are to be spiritually healthy, they must learn to feed themselves, too. The word of God is the word of life. How embarrassing it would have been had my 18-year-old daughter never learned to feed herself. Can you imagine me showing up at noon at the university cafeteria to scoop peas into her mouth in front of all the other students? But some people who have been Christians for decades still have not learned to feed themselves spiritually!

Have you ever considered what things last forever? Many things in which we invest a great deal of time and money will not last beyond the grave. Houses, cars, and jobs do not last beyond the grave. Junkyards are full of things that are rotting and rusting away—temporary things. Only three things last beyond the grave: God, God's word, and people. Isaiah 40:8 says, "The grass withers and the flowers fall, but the word of our God stands forever." Because the word of God lasts forever, investing significant time and effort in reading and studying it makes good sense.

The first step in becoming spiritually nourished is actually reading the Bible regularly. Sometimes the most powerful ideas are the simplest. One of my doctoral program professors, Dr. Plueddemann, said something that changed my daily habits. He described how he read the Bible first in the morning—before turning on the computer or the television or reading anything else, such as a newspaper. *Bible first* is a simple, yet a life-changing, principle.

I love the picture Psalm 1:1–3 presents: A man who meditates on God's Word day and night is pictured as a fruitful tree that has put down deep roots near life-giving water. In much the same way, Henri Nouwen's writings challenge me to meditate and "chew on" short phrases of Scripture. I took the well-known phrase "The Lord is my shepherd" and meditated on it one day during every possible moment. My spiritual roots grew deep as I drew into my soul the truth of that verse. Each of the words of that short phrase is pregnant with life. In fact, I once heard a preacher preach a five-point sermon emphasizing the meaning of each word in turn:

The Lord is my shepherd. (He is the only God; there is no other.)

The *Lord* is my shepherd. (He is sovereign over my life.)

The Lord *is* my shepherd. (Right now, in the present.)

The Lord is *my* shepherd. (He knows my name, and he cares about me personally.)

The Lord is my *shepherd*. (He tenderly leads me to pasture and to water, protecting me just as a shepherd protects his sheep.)

Feeding on the word of God is necessary, but true spiritual nourishment doesn't come from merely reading the Bible or even from memorizing it—we must apply its meaning to our lives, obeying its commands.

When the Bible uses the word *know* or *knowledge*, it usually is not talking about head knowledge or knowing a collection of facts. Rather, it is talking about "experiential knowledge" or "relational knowledge." In other words, there is a difference in *knowing about Jesus* and *knowing Jesus*. The relational intimacy the Bible talks about using the word *know* can include the idea of sexual intimacy in marriage, as when Genesis says that Adam *knew* Eve (as translated in the King James Version). The concept of knowing someone intimately can help us get a handle on what it means to be spiritually nourished. In his book *Not a Fan*, preacher Kyle Idleman wrote that Jesus is not looking for fans. Rather, he is looking for passionate, intimate, obedient followers. Being nourished by the written word of God must also include having a relationship with Jesus, the living word of God.

James 4:17 says, "Anyone, then, who knows the good he ought to do and *doesn't do it*, sins." This is one of the most sobering Scriptures in the entire Bible. Think of how many sermons you have heard, how many Bible lessons you have heard, that you didn't apply to your life. Indeed, lack of application is one of my greatest fears about teaching and preaching. Someone can easily thank me for a good sermon or lesson, then walk to the car, drive home, eat lunch, take a nap, and do nothing about what he or she learned through it. So when I led a small group in our home a few years ago, I decided not to pick a curriculum or a book to go through. Rather, we talked about Sunday's sermon and discussed how we could apply its teaching to our lives.

During my first ministry as a small town youth minister, I thought about all the different messages that the kids in my youth group received in a relatively short amount of time, and I counted the possibility for up to four different messages in the space of twelve hours. On a typical Sunday, they might hear a lesson about *prayer* in the high school Sunday school class, then a sermon on *grace* during the regular church service. That night, they would hear another sermon, this time about *repentance*—and then, during our youth group meeting, they might take part in a discussion about *witnessing*. In the space of twelve hours, they could hear as many as four different messages. But actually they would have heard only one message: *You don't have to stop and take the time to apply this to your life, because if you wait a few minutes, you'll hear another message.* After realizing this, I tried to focus on a single topic for an entire month in my youth programming, approaching it from different angles but always focusing on how to apply it in life. Some have said about Christians that "we already know a lot more than we are doing." A professor colleague of mine once referred to our constant taking in of biblical knowledge without applying it to our lives as *spiritual constipation*. It's as if we pull up to a gas station but keep putting gas in the car after the tank is full, spilling fuel everywhere and creating a dangerous situation.

My wife and I learned to speak Swahili in the DR Congo using a self-directed language learning method called LAMP, which helps people learn a second language the same way we learned our mother tongue when we were babies. The method is simple: Learn a little, and use it a lot. This approach is opposite of the one taken by today's educational system, in which going to school is like trying to drink from an open fire hydrant, with negligible time remaining for assimilation and application. I think we should learn the Bible the same way we learned our mother tongue: Learn a little and use it a lot, making it part of our core knowledge, keeping it from going in one ear and out the other.

I have tried to memorize Philippians 4:4–9, a powerful passage of Scripture. I find that meditating on the passage changes how I think and feel—even how I see the world. "The word of God is living and active," "sharper than any two edged sword" (Heb 4:12). To help me learn to use it, I borrowed an idea from Billy Graham that has made the Bible part of my daily life. Billy puts an open Bible on a table or counter in his house so that whenever he walks by, he can easily stop and read it. I decided to do this in my office at school: I leave an open Bible atop a small bookcase, open to the phrase on which I am trying to meditate that day. As I go through my day, I take moments all day long to read the phrase from the open Bible, thinking about its live-giving truth.

Right now, my daily Bible reading plan follows seven bookmarks in my Bible. I read one of Proverbs' thirty-one chapters each day of the month. I read one of Psalms's 150 chapters every day, completing the entire book every five months. I read a passage from the Old Testament, one from the Gospels, one from the book of Acts, one from the book of Revelation, and one from the remainder of the New Testament. Except when reading Psalms and Proverbs, I read just enough of a passage to have read something on which to reflect. Sometimes I read only one verse—sometimes a whole chapter. That's because Bible-in-a-year plans don't work very well for me. When I try them, I find myself reading only to make up lost ground, because I've gotten behind the schedule. I also find myself without enough time to reflect on what I've read and consider how to apply it. Reading from seven different sections of the Bible helps me eat a more balanced spiritual meal, and it gives me time to digest my spiritual food. After reading, I usually write a prayer to God in my journal, using material from the passages I have just read.

I'm not a big fan of tattoos. I wonder: *Are you sure you'll want that on your skin when you are seventy or eighty years old?* But I make an exception for

Scriptural tattoos, which seem to recall the Bible's insistence that we take the commands of God and "tie them as symbols on your hands and bind them on your foreheads" (Deut 6:8) and "bind them on your fingers; write them on the tablet of your heart" (Prov 7:3). One student of mine has her arm tattooed with a picture of a tree and the words "abide in me," from John 15; another student simply has the word "beloved" tattooed on her arm, from 1 John 3:1.

In one of the last letters Paul wrote before dying, he told Timothy, "All Scripture is God-breathed and is useful for teaching, rebuking, correcting and training in righteousness, so that the man of God may be thoroughly equipped for every good work." (2 Tim 3:16–17)

The word of God is the bread of life. We have no excuse not to be spiritually well-fed followers of Jesus. We have many versions of the Bible in our mother tongue, but it's time that we read them, reflect on what they say, and get some tattoos on our hearts.

LIFE APPLICATION

1. Create a simple, doable Bible reading plan for yourself. Consider writing prayers to God that come directly from your Bible reading.
2. Put the Bible first—before Facebook, Instagram, television, radio, or newspaper. Consider limiting your time with social media to make sure that you are being spiritually nourished.
3. Pick a phrase of Scripture on which to meditate, then chew on it all day long. Put it where you will constantly see it—on your fridge, dashboard, mirror, cell phone, or so forth.

CHAPTER 18

THE PRAYING LIFE

Life is too short not to converse with God

"Pray continually."
1 Thessalonians 5:17

"Because we have such a short time to live,
we should spend our remaining time with God."
Brother Lawrence

Because we will be talking with God for eternity, it makes sense for us to begin our conversation with him while we are on Earth. We should start these daily conversations the moment we wake up. Our first thoughts should be a prayer instead of us reviling the alarm clock or begging for caffeine. Consider this morning prayer of John Baille:

Eternal Father of my soul,
Let my first thought today be of You,
Let my first impulse be to worship You,

Let my first speech be Your name,
Let my first action be to kneel before You in prayer.

One of the greatest struggles of living the praying life comes every morning, when we first wake up and all our fears and anxieties and the demands of the day come rushing into our consciousness. We need to develop a habit that helps us begin a conversation with the Lord the moment we wake up, then carry on this conversation with him throughout the entire day. At night, just before our head hits the pillow, we can say, "Thank you, Lord, for walking with me through this day. Good night—I'll talk to you again first thing in the morning."

I have adopted a new prayer habit. I got the idea from watching my grandson Everett, when he was about 2 years old. My wife had bought him a cute little pair of rain boots, the kind with two little handles at the top that help you pull them on. Everett liked wearing his boots, but he often stumbled and fell when trying to walk too quickly in them. When I was with him while he was wearing his boots, I would often say, "Now, hold onto Grandpa's hand so we can walk without falling." One day, I reflected on this as a picture of me and God—I am the stumbling toddler, and God is offering to reach down and hold my hand and walk beside me. So now, most mornings, when I sit on the edge of the bed before standing up, I reach up with one of my hands and ask the Lord to hold my hand as I begin another day's walk with him. The first thing in the morning is a good time to ask for the day's marching orders. We need to let the Lord know that we are ready to be led by him and used by him, asking him to tell us *his* agenda for the day.

If we are to start each day this way, prayer must become one of our life's highest priorities instead of a last resort. I confess that sometimes, after trying everything else, I have said something like "Well—I guess all we can do now is pray." My friend David Butts likens this bad theology to a soldier lamenting his lack of a good weapon before he goes into battle: "I don't have a machine gun or a hand grenade or even a good knife," says the soldier. "All

I have is this nuclear bomb." Saying "I guess all we can do now is pray" is as good as saying, "All we can do now is tap into the power of the one who made the universe."

We also must stop thinking about prayer as preparation for something else. Oswald Chambers said, "Prayer does not fit us for the greater works; prayer *is* the greater work." We pray before we do many things. We pray before we eat a meal, travel, or teach a class. Somehow we need to develop the habit of *praying first* at other times as well, including during times of medical crisis. Many American Christians do a lot of things early on when they get sick—head to the medicine cabinet, visit the doctor, or even call 911. These are not bad things, but perhaps they shouldn't always be the very first thing we do. James tells us that anyone who is sick should call the elders of the church to pray over him or her (Jas 5:14).

A pastor who is a good friend of mine told a story illustrating how we prioritize prayer. In front of the church where he served, a vehicle that had been turning in the intersection had crashed, throwing out its window a passenger who had not been wearing a seat belt. My friend and several others heard the sounds of the accident and came running to help. After someone had called 911, as they were waiting for the ambulance to arrive, a lady put her hand on my friend's shoulder and quietly asked, "Shouldn't we pray?" My friend told me how convicted and humbled he had been by the woman's words. He was a pastor; why hadn't he thought of praying?

When prayer becomes our priority, we begin praying for everyone we know. Paul insisted to Timothy that "requests, prayers, intercession and thanksgiving be made for *everyone*" (1 Tim 2:1). In the next verse, we see that Paul even includes pagan kings. When George W. Bush was elected president of the United States, a group of evangelical Christians tried to get a million Christians to pray for him every day. It sounded like a great thing to do, but I felt a nagging conviction from the Lord, as if he were saying to me, "Mike, why didn't you pray for Bill Clinton? I heard you laugh at a lot of Bill and Hillary jokes, but I didn't ask you to joke about the president—I asked you to pray for him!" It felt like a kick in the gut from the Holy Spirit.

The Bible doesn't tell us to pray only for people we like—it tells us to pray for *everyone*. Jesus told his followers to pray for their enemies, including those who persecute them (Matt 5:44). Howard Crowl, one of my missionary colleagues in the DR Congo, gave me some great advice about prayer. A certain Congolese pastor, he said, had always irritated him by his words and actions. Howard realized that he was in danger of developing bitterness and resentment toward the man, so he intentionally began to pray for the man by name—every day. Howard was not praying because he *wanted to*; he prayed because he knew he *needed to*, regardless of whether he felt like doing so. Howard illustrated to me by putting his fingers on his lips and forcibly moving his lips, saying: "I will pray for this man every day, even if I have to *make myself pray by moving my lips*!"

Have you ever wondered why God wants us to pray when he already knows what we need and what we are thinking? The answer may be found in parent–child relationships. God is our heavenly Father, and we are his children. I hate when our children go from being small, wanting to share every detail in their life and hearts, to a time in life when it isn't "cool" to talk to your parents. I have had "conversations" with one of my teenagers that went something like this:

Mike: "How are you doing today?"
Teen: "Fine."
Mike: "What happened at school today?"
Teen: "Nothing."
Mike: "What are your plans for this week?"
Teen: "Don't know."

This has always frustrated me, because I love my kids, and I want them to always talk to me.

I know that God knows everything, but I think he still enjoys hearing his children's voices when they talk to him. Parents don't like nagging, whining, and demanding voices, but I love it when one of my children, worried or fearful or confused, comes to me in a soft, humble voice and says, "Daddy, can you help me? I really need your help!" Other times, when I know they need my help and encouragement, and when I want more than anything to give it to them—I wait for them to admit it and ask for help. Jesus tells us to ask, seek, and knock (see Matt 7:7)—our heavenly father is not slow to hear our requests, nor reluctant to respond to them.

God wants his children to talk to him about *everything*. Indeed, Brother Lawrence challenged us to not limit in any way our conversations with God. No topic is off limits:

The most holy and necessary practice in our spiritual life is the presence of God. That means finding constant pleasure in His divine company, speaking humbly and lovingly with Him in all seasons, at every moment, without limiting the conversation in any way. This is especially important in times of temptation, sorrow, separation from God, and even in times of unfaithfulness and sin.

It is ridiculous for us to think that we can hide anything from God. Because God already knows every one of our impure thoughts or selfish desires, talking to him about them makes perfect sense. A book about fighting sexual temptation contained some very transparent prayers, prayed by the author, that encouraged me to talk to God directly in moments of temptation. Can you imagine praying a prayer something like this?

Father God, I see that woman over there wearing the short skirt and the low-cut blouse. Everything in me wants to stare at her lustfully. By the way, you really knew what you were doing when you created the female body—wow! It seems as if staring at her will bring pleasure and fulfillment, but I know where this leads. It will only take me down the dark road of nonfulfillment, causing me to crave more. I really need your help right now. Please help me redirect my thoughts to the beautiful wife you have given me.

Remind me that she is my one and only—the legitimate place for real sexual fulfillment. Help me right now, Lord, in this moment!

Perhaps talking to God about such things might seem undignified or irreverent. But God knows you even better than you know yourself (see Ps 139), and he greatly desires to change you to make you more like Jesus. Knowing that, this kind of praying makes perfect sense.

Prayer is a two-way conversation. It is asking, but it is also listening. At times in my life, God has spoken to me so clearly, in such a compelling way, that his voice came very close to being audible. Once this happened when I was 21 years old, very self-righteous in my belief that I belonged to the "right church" and had the "right theology." I was attending a retreat with many other Christians hailing from different denominations, and the Lord made it very clear to me that I had much *to learn* from Baptists and Pentecostals—if I would only humble myself. Another time, I heard the Lord clearly telling me in my spirit to become a father to a fatherless girl. I also heard the inner voice of the Lord, speaking clearly and powerfully, when I asked him to tell me what he thought of me. He told me how much he loved me—how precious I was to him.

Brother Lawrence calls the praying life "the practice of the presence of God." Life is too short not to talk to someone who is always with us.

LIFE APPLICATION

1. What morning habit can you create that will help you begin a conversation with God the moment you wake up?
2. What reminders can you put in your daily life to remind you of God's presence? How can you use pictures of people or sticky notes to trigger intercessory prayer?
3. When you pray, make a habit of stopping and listening for at least as long as you speak.

CHAPTER 19

THE GROWN-UP LIFE

Life is too short to keep thinking like a child

*"When I was a child, I talked like a child, I
thought like a child, I reasoned like a child. When
I became a man, I put childish ways behind me."*
1 Corinthians 13:11

"Everyone is a grown-up child."
Anonymous

Everyone is just a grown-up kid. We all carry a little boy or little girl around inside our adult bodies. Sometimes that angry, confused, or hurt little boy or girl comes out in our adult life and causes problems in how we think and act. Recently, one of my university students was given an interesting assignment by her counselor. The counselor asked her to write a letter to her younger self to help heal the little girl she carried around inside of her, a girl who had been abused at an early age. I was so inspired by her letter that I decided to write one to the "little Mike" I have carried around inside for over sixty years:

Dear little Mike,

I know you have worried about being incompetent at doing things like mechanics and building construction. You need to know your older brother Dave was only trying to bolster his own ego when he told you that you weren't good with your hands. You do go on to become pretty good at building and fixing things. Yes, your brother grew up to become an amazing carpenter and contractor, but you got pretty good at some stuff, too. I'll be honest—you do still struggle with mechanics, but that's okay; you can always pay to have someone else work on your car.

I know that you haven't always felt very smart, even when you got straight A's on your report card. I know you will never forget the times when Dad was trying to tell you how to do something and you got so flustered that you kept messing it up, and then Dad would yell, "Don't think, just do what I say!" I know you wondered at the time if you were too stupid to even think. Well, guess what? If you just hang in there until you are 55, you will actually earn a Ph.D. in intercultural studies. And, by the way, they don't just hand those out to stupid people.

I know you are both very interested in and scared to death of girls right now. You need to know you will eventually marry a beautiful, amazing girl from Canada, and you are now in your fourth decade of marriage! You have a great marriage, but I need to confess that you probably won't ever truly understand girls or women; they will continue to be one of the greatest mysteries of your life.

I know you have worried about your body and whether you would grow up to be a strong and healthy man. I know that it is embarrassing right now to sit at the lunch table with your first girlfriend, Donna, since she is five feet, two inches tall and you are only four feet, eight inches! You do grow taller; you will eventually reach five feet, ten inches and even have a son named Jason who is over six feet tall, whom you affectionately nicknamed LBJ, for "little buddy Jason."

I know you often wonder about what kind of job you will have in life and whether you will be able to ever get a job. Well, by age 61, you have had four amazing occupations so far: a youth minister, a missionary to the DR Congo, a university professor, and a local church teaching pastor. You have been teaching at a Christian university for the last twenty-five years, and you still can't believe they pay you to do this, because you love it so much.

I know you are concerned about your looks and whether you will ever be considered handsome. And I know you hate wearing glasses. You will eventually be able to wear contacts, which help some; and believe it or not, you will learn to like wearing your trifocal glasses. Your hair will turn white or gray pretty quickly, but guess what—you get to keep it! No walking around dealing with baldness like other guys!

I know you walk around sometimes wondering if there will be a nuclear war, and you even have nightmares about it sometimes. Believe it or not, the "evil" Soviet Union will eventually break apart, and there will be no more Cold War. A pretty scary day does come when you are 43, when some Muslim extremists hijack planes and attack buildings full of people in New York City and Washington, D.C. That begins an ongoing "war on terrorism." I guess there will always be something like this to worry about until Jesus comes back and stops all the bad stuff.

I know you have felt verbally and emotionally abused by Dad. Well, he's still Dad, but at 83, he has mellowed out some. He softened a bit after losing mom a couple of years ago and he even has a certain tenderness about him sometimes when talking with his grandkids and great-grandkids. I know you have worried a lot about his marriage to Mom, especially when Dad is yelling at Mom and she is always pushing his buttons. Guess what? Somehow they stuck with it and were married for over 60 years. One of the coolest things, though, is that God has given you three amazing children who marry wonderful spouses and three precious grandchildren. God has allowed you to begin to break the generational cycle of abuse in your family. God has also given you a ministry to the fatherless that come into your life. Your love for the fatherless continues to grow and you have played the role of a loving father figure to many young people who needed a good dad.

I know you feel ashamed about the sexual abuse you have endured from John. I know that right now you are still confused about what happened to you and that you feel very dirty and ashamed about it. I want you to know that nothing about what happened was your fault—none of it! When you reach your forties, you will finally begin to tell others about it. You talked to a good Christian counselor about it, and you even speak about it sometimes in sermons and lessons now. Believe it or not, you are even ready to meet and talk to John if the opportunity presents itself. You have forgiven him, but you are also ready to confront him about the truth of what happened and to help make sure he doesn't do this to any other young boys.

I know what happened inside you that day you went to play basketball in the driveway of your friend Brad's house. You will probably never forget going in his dad's garage and seeing the calendar pictures of naked women on the wall. I know that day was the beginning of a lifelong struggle with the desire to look at more pictures of naked women as they became available. Fortunately, it was kind of hard to find pictures like that when you were in junior high and high school. You really got blindsided, though, when they invented the Internet when you were in your thirties. I want you to know that even though the normal temptation to lust is still there, God has shown you how to wisely fight this addiction. He has taught you about safe boundaries and the power of confession and accountability with other men. He is teaching you how to use this broken area of your life to your spiritual advantage—a constant reminder that you desperately need Jesus every hour and every minute.

You are at a point now where, because of the Lord's grace and power, you can claim victory over the compulsive addiction you struggled with for many years. Jesus is using your willingness to be transparent about your brokenness and struggle in this area as a tool of ministry to help others. Many young men (and some young women) at the Christian university where you teach have been coming to you for help. These students walk around in a world so different from the "pinup calendar world" you encountered at 10 years old. Because of the Internet and smartphones, pornography is now easily accessible, very affordable (much of it for free), and anonymous. These students really need your help. Your love for God and your honest, transparent struggle is giving you a platform of credibility with them. You have started a sharing and discussion time in the men's dorm called the "Master's Men." You and other older men are dealing transparently with issues like this, challenging younger men to truly live as bondservants of Jesus.

I will leave you with a truth from Scripture: "He who began a good work in you will carry it on to completion until the day of Christ Jesus" (Phil 1:6). Hang in there, little Mike—you are going to make it!

Sincerely, older Mike

Life is too short to allow childish thoughts to dominate our adult lives. It is time for us all to grow up and become true adults who talk, think, and reason like mature adults. May the truth set us free from childish thoughts and fears!

LIFE APPLICATION

1. Do some personal introspection. What negative defining moments and negative scripts from your childhood do you still carry around inside yourself today?

2. Ask God to show you some of the "childish reactions" you commonly have when you are stressed out by something or someone.

3. Sit down and write a letter of advice and encouragement to the little child you carry around inside you.

CHAPTER 20

THE PRESENT LIFE

Life is too short not to be fully present where you are

"This is the day the Lord has made; let us rejoice and be glad in it."
Psalm 118:24

"Therefore do not worry about tomorrow, for tomorrow will worry about itself. Each day has enough trouble of its own."
Matthew 6:34

One day when my daughter Sammy was three, I was holding her on my hip. We were standing in the dining room of our home, and she was trying to tell me something important—but she could tell that I was looking away at something else. So she grabbed both of my cheeks with her little hands, jerked my head around to look directly at her, and said, "Daddy, I am *talking* to you!" I wish I could say that I learned my lesson that day, but my adult children and my wife still tell me sometimes that I'm not paying attention when they talk to me.

Nor will I forget the time when an older gentleman firmly rebuked me for my lack of attention to my own family. Rees Bryant, a professor in the graduate school at the university where I teach, was the consummate southern gentleman. Because he was such a kind and gentle man, his conversation with me took me off guard. He started by asking me how things were going in my local church in Mt. Pulaski, Illinois, where he knew I had been serving as an elder. I responded that I had been working hard as an elder and told him that things were mostly going okay, with a few bumps here and there. He then looked me in the eye and said, "Mike, I think there are probably a lot of other men in Mt. Pulaski who could do as good a job as you—or a better job than you—as an elder." His statement surprised and confused me. Then he asked me how I was doing as a missions/intercultural studies professor in the undergraduate school. I told him that I was working hard and that the number of students in our program was growing. He looked me in the eye again and said, "Mike, I think there are probably a lot of other men who could do as good a job as you—or a better job than you—as a missions professor." Shocked by his words, I wondered what in the world was he trying to tell me. His next statement hit me right between the eyes: "Mike, there is only one man in all the world God has called to be Julie's husband and Sarah, Jason, and Sammy's daddy, and *that is you*. And *you can't be replaced!*" He had set me up for the punch line, and indeed—it felt like a punch in the gut. The brevity of life should remind us to be fully present with others in life, especially our family.

Part of the problem in our culture is our extreme future orientation. We don't have time to enjoy today, because we are always thinking about tomorrow. One indication of our future orientation is how much money we spend on insurance of every kind. There is wisdom in being insured for the future, but sometimes it can make us focus on future negative scenarios, robbing us of today's joy. Have you caught yourself playing the "What If" game? *What if this happens? What will I do?* In this mind game, we constantly replay various negative scenarios that might come to pass. This game keeps us from enjoying the present. Having entered the empty nest season of life, I often forget that it could be one of the most special times of my married life. If I can pay full attention to my wife, this season can become just as enjoyable as it was being newlyweds.

Another mind game we often play is the "When Then" game: *When I get that better job or that new house, then I will be happy.* This game may sound a little more positive than the "What If" game, but it still keeps your thoughts focused in the future, not in the present. We can easily forget that we are living, right now, in the time we will probably someday call the "good ole days." I was surprised, watching the final TV episode of *The Office*, when one of the actors asked, "Why can't we realize we are actually in the 'good ole days' when we are in them?" Why? Because we are not fully present in the present, enjoying the beauty and blessing of *now*. We do have the power to be fully present now and to decide to be happy now, leaving the future up to God. Indeed, James warns us about living too far in the future:

Now listen, you who say, "Today or tomorrow we will go to this or that city, spend a year there, carry on business and make money." Why, you do not even know what will happen tomorrow. What is your life? You are a mist that appears for a little while and then vanishes. (Jas 4:13–14)

The past also distracts us from the present. People who struggle with guilt allow their past to define them. I will never forget a hard conversation I had with Julie during our second term of service in the DR Congo. When I came home one night, she gave me a serious look and said, "We have to talk." It was the kind of comment that makes most men shudder, thinking *What have I done? What am I in trouble for now?* After putting the kids to bed, we sat down, and Julie looked directly at me and said, "Mike, I know that you love me and the kids, but I need to be honest: When you come home at night, it is like you are not even here—you have nothing left for us." Her statement hit me hard, because I knew it was true. After considering why I had been working too hard, I realized that I had been subconsciously reacting to my past. On an emotional level, I had been working to please my father—and he wasn't even living in the DR Congo at the time! I was allowing my past to negatively affect my present.

I am trying to remind myself to be more mindful in everything I do. I know that many ordinary things hold beauty that I can see if I train myself to pay attention to them. Think of how many times we walk past flowers every day without taking the time to see them, let alone smell them. Taking time to smell the roses should not just be a saying: It should be a basic rule of life. How many beautiful sunsets have we missed because we were watching television or were distracted, thinking about something else while driving our car? How many precious little children have we ignored in our rush to get to the next thing on our agenda? Think of the all the times we have been with the people we love the most but have taken them for granted, not paying attention to them and expressing our love in the moment. Seeing the beauty in ordinary things is a learned discipline, as is taking the time to appreciate the beauty of nature or the beauty of a person. If you are willing to take the time and pay attention, you can see beauty in every person you meet, even the grumpy ones.

I am trying to be more present in everything I do, both when I am at work and when I am at play. I have started being more present when I eat a meal as well. Indeed, being mindful of what I am eating and how I am eating it brings many benefits. Slowing down to taste food is a way to enjoy it more in the present as well as a way to eat more healthfully. If I am fully present when eating, I will know when my hunger is satisfied, not falling into mindless overeating just because something tastes good. Being fully present is also a basic safety precaution. Have you ever cut yourself with a knife because you weren't paying attention to what you were doing? Similarly, many car accidents happen simply because a driver was not fully present while driving. When driving on a long trip, how frightening it is to try to remember things you saw the previous ten minutes of driving, only to realize that there is nothing there to remember—your brain was on autopilot.

Relationally and spiritually, we can benefit by being fully present in our emotions. Identifying the emotion we are feeling in the present will help us make wise choices when we respond to others and will allow us to know how to pray about what we are feeling.

When I was looking at some old photos of my kids the other day, I felt a twinge of sadness and regret come over me. I realized how often I hadn't been fully present when they were growing up—and I had no way of going back and doing it again. I want my sadness to be a wakeup call, calling me to be fully present now in their lives. No time is too late a time to start paying attention or to be fully present. Moreover, I am trying harder to be fully present when I talk with people. Proverbs 18:13 says, "He who answers before listening—that is his folly and his shame." I am ashamed when I think of all the times when I have caught myself trying to think about what I am going to say next in a conversation instead of being fully present and listening to the other person.

Right now, you are somewhere. Life is too short not to be fully present, fully enjoying where you are right now.

LIFE APPLICATION

1. What can you do to remind yourself to be fully present? Make a habit of looking at people when you talk to them. Stop yourself from thinking about what you are going to say next while someone else is speaking to you.

2. What distracts you the most from the present—the future, or the past? What practical thing can you do to remove this distraction?

3. What things do you consider truly beautiful? How can you put more of these beautiful things into your daily life? When you see something ordinary or even ugly, try to find something beautiful in it. Ask God to help you develop an eye for the wonders of creation—everything from tiny snowflakes to enormous mountain ranges.

Part Two

The *SHORT LIFE*
Impacts Your Outer World

CHAPTER 21

THE REGRETLESS LIFE

Life is too short to live with regrets

> *"Now I know that none of you of whom I have gone about*
> *preaching the kingdom will ever see me again. Therefore, I declare*
> *to you today that I am innocent of the blood of all men. For I*
> *have not hesitated to proclaim to you the whole will of God."*
> **Acts 20:25–27**

> *"No reserves, no retreats, no regrets."*
> **William Borden**

One of the saddest things would be getting to the end of your life only to say, "I sensed that God wanted me to do something significant with my life, but I was afraid that I would never be able to do it, so I took the safe route." William Borden was only 25 years old when he died of meningitis in Egypt, where he was preparing himself to be a missionary in the Muslim world. A quote found written in his Bible—"No reserves, no retreats, no regrets"—demonstrated that he had indeed counted the cost: that he had no regrets about the life decisions he had made. I want to live like William Borden—having no regrets.

One of first times I remember feeling regret was in junior high school. I had gone to the county fair, and my dad had given me $10. He warned me not to spend it quickly—it was supposed to last me the whole day. I think he even said something about spending it wisely and having something to show for it at the end of the day. But I wasn't listening very well, for I was mesmerized by the carnival hawkers and all their booths. I could grab a treasure using the cranked claw. I could get my girlfriend a stuffed animal by pitching a baseball into a stack of milk cans. And tossing coins into glass cups and dishes looked so easy that I knew I could get something special for my mom. But within the first hour, I had spent all my money, and I had nothing to show for it. I regretted how quickly I had spent the money, but too late—now it was all gone.

I learned a hard lesson about regret from our last dog, Holly, a beautiful golden retriever. She had been a great source of joy for our family, but she needed to be put to sleep, because her health was failing. I had planned to say my goodbyes to Holly at the vet's office, where my wife had taken her for the procedure, but because of a miscommunication with my wife, I arrived too late. How I regretted missing the opportunity to say goodbye to her!

During college, I took the opportunity to leave no room for regrets when saying goodbye to a missionary woman named Carolyn, with whom I had grown very close during my senior year of college. She and her family were returning to the DR Congo to continue their missionary service. I had dated her daughter for a while, and she had become like a second mother to me. At a farewell party at her house, when it came time for me to leave, I gave her a brief side hug and then left. But as I drove away, I began to regret having given her such a casual hug, knowing that she was returning to Africa and that I wouldn't see her again for a long time. I thought about turning around, but going back and saying goodbye to her again seemed silly. Yet my feelings of regret were so strong that I turned the car around anyway and headed back to her house. When I came through the door again, she gave me a puzzled look, and I explained. Then I gave her a long, heartfelt embrace before leaving, this time with tears in my eyes. That hug meant a lot to her—and to me as well. I felt good having no regrets about how I had said goodbye.

Many times we don't get the chance to plan the goodbyes we say to people. When someone dies unexpectedly, living with regrets can be difficult, especially if you aren't happy with the last interaction you had with that person before he or she died. On February 22, 2013, a very special woman in my life, Iva Speece, died of a massive stroke. Iva had been a second mother to me since my high school days. My brother had married her oldest daughter, I had dated her youngest daughter and our families had always been very close. I was with her a few days before her death, at her grandson's (my nephew's) senior night basketball game. I hugged her when I first saw her, and I sat in front of her at the basketball game, but for some reason I didn't talk to her very much that night. We all went out for pizza after the game, but I was in a hurry to get home, so we didn't stay long. As we were leaving, I waved at everyone and took off without giving anyone goodbye hugs. Had I known that night was my last chance to talk to Iva, I would have hugged her and told her how much she meant to me. I regret that I didn't do that, because a couple days later, she died.

You never know when your last conversation with someone will be. I rushed to see Iva in the hospital when I heard about the stroke, but she was nonresponsive, unable to talk with anyone. My youngest daughter Sammy, however, had had a different experience with Iva at my nephew's basketball gave. She told me about an awesome last conversation she had with Iva, in which she told Iva how growing up, she always thought that Iva was her grandmother. Because Iva always seemed to be at family functions, and because Iva was her cousin's grandma, Sammy just assumed that Iva was her grandma, too. Sammy could tell that what she said really blessed Iva, who smiled a big smile and told Sammy that she would love to consider Sammy one of her grandkids.

My father-in-law died from a stroke about the same time as Iva did. He lived in Ontario, Canada, and we were unable to go see him before he passed away. I feel regret when I think about my interactions with him after I married his daughter. He was a gruff man and was hard to talk to. He was a farmer, a horse-breeder, and an auto body repairman. We never seemed to have much in common to talk about when we were together, and due to Julie's and my decade of missionary work in Africa—and our life in Illinois after that—I wasn't able to see him much. Whenever we were together, we always had surface conversations about things that really didn't matter. I prayed for him often, but what I regret the most is that I never found a way to talk to him about Jesus. When I heard that he had died, I felt a deep twinge of regret. Regret always feels bitter, because you know that you no longer have the chance to go back and do something that you now wish you had done.

I love the song "Slip on By," by Finding Favor, which tells the story of an old man fishing by the riverside who struck up a conversation with a young man next to him. The old man tells the young man about all the things he regrets having missed in his life. He doesn't know where all the time has gone: He feels as if he just woke up and found himself 83 years old. He wishes he had held his young bride when they first fought, wishes he hadn't hung up the telephone on his mother the day she died, and regrets not spending time playing with his son when he was young—not least because his son grew up, went to war, and died. He says that what hurts the most is knowing what could have been. This song teaches the truth that since God gives us only so much precious time on earth, we have to make sure we don't let it slip on by.

An old man who once toured a Wycliffe Bible Translators center in North Carolina listened to the tour guide talk about the Bibleless peoples of the world, describing how translators were giving their lives to translate God's world into the heart language of these peoples. The tour guide related how their doing so was transforming whole villages and people groups. During a question-and-answer session at the end of the tour, the old man raised his hand and asked, with tears in his eyes, "What do you do when you are 80 years old and for the first time in your life, you've heard about something worth giving your life to?" Of course, the answer is that you start giving your life to things that matter whatever your age. You are never too late to start honoring God with your life, even if you have only a few days, hours, or minutes remaining.

John Piper writes, in his book *Don't Waste Your Life*, about something he calls a tragedy. In *The Reader's Digest*, he read about a couple who had retired early from their jobs in the northeast, when they were in their fifties. They went to live in Florida, where they spent their days cruising on their boat, playing softball, and collecting shells. Piper pictured them standing before Christ at the great day of judgment, showing him what they had done with their lives: "Look, Lord—see my pretty shells."

I have struggled a lot with the concept of retirement, which I believe is a cultural construct of American society tied to the so-called American dream. Everyone seems to dream about the day when he or she can quit working, sit back, and enjoy life. I am not against changing jobs when you get older, especially to work at something that is less physically or emotionally demanding. Certainly a decline in physical strength is normal as we get older, but I love those older people who say things such as "I'm not retiring—just being redeployed!" I also love meeting older people who have figured out that life is not about them, but rather about serving God and others. How wonderful when retirees figure out how to focus on things that are connected to their gifts and calling in the later years of their lives: They are living the regretless life.

The purpose of life is not to work hard so that you can retire. The purpose of life is not to make paychecks and spend paychecks, then repeat this cycle over and over until you die. The purpose of life is to serve God until your final breath—then worship him for eternity.

We invited Professor Rob Gallagher from Wheaton College to preach and share with our students at Lincoln Christian University. One night, during a question-and-answer session in the student center, Rob reflected on times in his life when he had to decide between two different paths. Looking backward, he saw how blessed he had been each time he chose the harder, riskier path. He said that if he had chosen the easier path, he would have regretted it. What he said reminded me of the famous lines in Robert Frost's poem: "Two roads diverged in a wood, and I—I took the one less traveled by. And that has made all the difference."

In the last chapter of this book I will talk about another LCU student, Sam VanGieson, who died from cancer at age 26. I went to Sam's funeral, which was held in our school chapel. I experienced a range of emotions as I heard different people give testimonies about Sam's life. There was much laughter and many tears. But the biggest emotion I felt that day was regret. Even though Sam didn't attend my classes, I deeply regretted not spending time with him or getting to know him. I prayed for Sam when our dean of students sent out health updates. I smiled and waved at him if I saw him on the sidewalk. But I never took the time to sit down and have a good conversation with him, and I sincerely regret that. I do still have a chance to get to know his widow, Savanah, better, and I want to make the most of that opportunity.

One of the things motivating me to finish writing this book is my desire to have no regrets about not getting it done before I die. You don't usually hear people regretting having taken some risks in life. I have, however, heard people share their wish to have taken more risks instead of always playing it safe. Brennan Manning's grandmother used to say, "To live without risk is to risk not living." Life is too short to live with regrets.

LIFE APPLICATION

1. Stop right now and ask yourself *If I were to die today, what regrets would I have?* Think about potential regrets having to do with all the roles you play in life and all the relationships you have.

2. What practical things can you do to address these potential regrets? Make a list, and start checking off its items.

3. What have you been thinking about doing for a while now that you need to simply get done before you regret having waited? If you had a bad argument with someone or lost your cool with someone, make amends quickly, before you are left with regrets.

CHAPTER 22

THE MARRIED LIFE

Life is too short to take your marriage for granted

"May you rejoice in the wife of your youth."
Proverbs 5:18

*"In marriage, the grass is not greener on the
other side—it is greener where you water it!"*
Unknown

L ife is too brief not to enjoy the time you are married. How amazing
that God gives many of us the opportunity, during our short time
on Earth, to get extremely close to another human being in the
context of a lifetime marriage covenant! Such a relationship is set apart for
deep intimacy in every area—physically, emotionally, mentally, spiritually.
The problem comes when we think that God gave us the institution of
marriage to make us happy. The truth? God knows how very selfish we all
are, and marriage is his best tool for revealing our basic selfishness. God
doesn't give us marriage to make us happy, he uses it to make us holy! God is

in the business of perfecting our character and making us ready for eternity in heaven with him.

Let me share some of my own marriage story. My grandmother always used to tell me, "You'd better look your best—you never know when you are going to meet your future wife." And she was right, on August 24, 1982—the first day I laid eyes on Julie, the woman who would become my life partner. I was walking down the sidewalk with one of my seminary friends when Julie and I crossed paths. When she passed by, I turned around to watch her walk away, exclaiming to my friend, "*Who* was *that?*" I asked her out on a date later that day, and in three days, I knew I wanted to marry her. We dated by telephone for a month while she was back home in Canada, and the next time I saw her in person, I asked her to marry me. She replied, "What took you so long?" We were married on December 4 that same year. Only three months and nine days after I first saw Julie, we walked down the aisle. (But I don't hold this up as a model for others to follow—especially when I'm talking to my kids!)

I don't believe that each person has one perfect match on the entire planet whom he or she must find, as if searching for a needle in a haystack. I do believe that God can guide people together, and I believe that he delights in giving his children good gifts. I believe that Julie was a direct gift from God in 1982—and yet I have taken her for granted many times during our thirty-seven years of marriage. And it's in just this regard that focusing on the brevity of life can help a marriage.

I remember the first time when I thought I might lose Julie. During our first year as missionaries in the DR Congo, she was pregnant, but before we could announce our pregnancy, Julie miscarried. I will never forget her urgent cry for help from the bathroom in the middle of the night. She wouldn't stop bleeding, and I raced across town to wake up Juanita, our missionary nurse, praying urgently all the way there and back—pleading and bargaining with God, terrified of losing my precious wife. Why do we fail to see someone's value until we nearly lose him or her?

Proverbs 5:18 reminds the husband to *rejoice* in the wife of his youth. The next verse goes on to emphasize permanence and longevity: "May her breasts satisfy you *always*, may you *ever* be captivated by her love." The author of Proverbs is calling a husband to rejoice in his wife as he did on his wedding day, no matter how long they have been married. Three strong principles arise from this passage of Scripture—*celebration*, *contentment*, and *captivation*—to help you value your spouse during the brief life we have been given.

Celebration should be tied to a person's unique existence. There are two basic ways of celebrating someone. Take our celebration of the anniversary of our day of birth. Birthdays are wonderful, meaningful events, because on them, we celebrate someone's existence. Such a celebration has nothing to do with physical appearance or achievements in life—a person is celebrated simply because *he or she is*. No one has to do anything to deserve a birthday celebration—just keep on breathing! A wise man or woman will communicate to his or her spouse, in both word and deed, "I celebrate YOU!"—with no "because" attached. Don't pick out things to celebrate about your spouse; rather, celebrate the mere fact of *his or her* existence.

Another effective way of celebrating your spouse is to focus on specific things that are unique and meaningful about your spouse's personality, physical appearance, and abilities. In our home, we have a family birthday tradition whereby each person shares one thing that he or she appreciates about the person whose existence we are celebrating. Receiving so many compliments can be a little embarrassing for that person—but he or she will long remember what was said and how good it made him or her feel. My wife explained to me once that she was grateful that I thanked her for things that she *did* for me—for example, cooking a delicious supper—but explained that she found such compliments less meaningful than when I highlighted something connected to her being: who she *was*. There is a subtle difference between saying "that was a great meal you just made" and "I think *you* are a great cook!" The first compliment focuses on the act, the second on the person. So for our twenty-fifth wedding anniversary, I tried something that brought great results. I wrote a short note every week for twenty-five weeks, listing twenty-five specific things I loved about Julie—things that were uniquely her, not just things she did for me. For example, some weeks I told her physical things I loved about her (her voice, her hair, her eyes), and other weeks I wrote about her personality traits (nature-lover, book-lover, laughs easily, and so forth). Blessed is the wife or husband whose spouse communicates in word and deed, "I celebrate YOU!"

Contentment is in short supply in our culture. Everywhere you look, people tell you to trade in your old model for a newer, "better" one. But the marriage covenant is a lifetime covenant, meant to be shared with only one person. Blessed is the wife or husband who is completely satisfied and contented with his or her spouse—for whom marriage is a truly safe place. Blessed is the wife who doesn't have to worry about pornography or about competition from other women, because her husband is a "one-woman man." Blessed is the husband who doesn't have to worry about being compared to other husbands or male co-workers. An old adage has it that "the grass is always greener on the other side," but a better saying would be that "the grass is always greener where you water it!"

The Proverbs five passage asks a rhetorical question: "Why embrace the bosom of *another man's wife?*" A key to contentment is realizing who actually fits into the category of "another man's wife." This category includes *all* 3.5 billion women on Earth, no matter their age. Every woman who is not already married is *potentially* the future wife of another man—and the same for goes for potential husbands. I once heard a marriage counselor say that after you get married, the question of whom to marry is no longer important—instead, the big question is how you treat the person to whom you are already married.

"Captivation" is a strong, passionate word—exactly the kind of word that describes how I felt when I first met and courted Julie. The question then becomes how a husband and a wife can maintain this kind of passion. Part of the solution is to *remember the feelings of the courtship days.* I carry a picture of Julie with me that was taken when she was 20, her age when I first met her. Sometimes just looking at this picture brings back those old feelings. I also find it helpful to *remember what you did when you were dating*. Someone has said that we have dating and marriage backward: We usually date so that we can get married, but we ought to be getting married so that we can date! Feelings follow actions. If you make a point of cherishing and treasuring your spouse, even when you don't feel like doing so, the captivating feelings will return.

Our home church in Mt. Pulaski, Illinois, was shocked in June 2006 at the sudden death of one of our staff members, Colleen McKinney. Colleen was only 44 years old, and she was probably the sweetest janitor our church had ever had. While she and her husband were riding their motorcycle one evening to Dairy Queen in Lincoln, Illinois, about twenty minutes from Mt. Pulaski, a young man in a pickup truck ran a stop sign and hit and killed Colleen. Sitting at the funeral, I was hit hard by the realization that Colleen was exactly the same age as my wife: They had been born just a month apart in 1961. Something about "dying on the way to Dairy Queen" kept ringing in my ear—*Julie could die at any time doing anything.* It was a wake-up call to celebrate the special gift God had given me in Julie. On his wedding day, Steve Szoke vowed to love his wife Candy "in sickness and in health." He didn't know that cancer would give him only twelve years of marriage. No spouse knows how long his or her marriage will be. Life is too brief to take your marriage for granted.

LIFE APPLICATION

1. How can you apply the lessons of Proverbs 5 to your own marriage? Think of a practical way of celebrating your spouse daily.

2. What can you do to remain contented and satisfied with your spouse? How can you communicate that you are not looking at the grass on the other side of the fence—because you are completely satisfied?

3. What can you do regularly (regardless of whether you feel like doing so) to demonstrate to your spouse that you treasure him or her?

Consider carrying a photograph of your spouse from when you were dating to help bring back thoughts and feelings from that time.

CHAPTER 23

THE SINGLE LIFE

Life is too short to waste your singleness

*"I would like for you to be free from concern. An unmarried man is
concerned about the Lord's affairs—how he can please the Lord.
An unmarried woman or virgin is concerned is about the Lord's affairs:
Her aim is to be devoted to the Lord in both body and spirit."*
Apostle Paul (1 Corinthians 7:32, 34)

L ife is too brief to be worried and dissatisfied during seasons of singleness. I was certainly not a satisfied single during my teenage years, nor into my early twenties. Looking back, I realize how desperate I was to find someone to love me—and how afraid that no one ever would. In high school, I was deathly afraid of girls. I had extreme difficulty talking to girls, let alone sticking out my neck enough to ask one on a date. Eventually I did date a girl—during my senior year of high school. She was a freshman, and I quizzed other friends mercilessly to be absolutely certain that she liked me before I mustered the courage to ask her out.

In college, I dated many different girls. But I had set myself up for a big let-down by assuming that I would meet my wife at the Christian college I was attending. You could say that my dating in college resembled the behavior of a small child chasing a butterfly. I jumped and grasped with all my might, but every beautiful butterfly was always just out of reach. Every relationship I began seemed to blow up in my face. Looking back, I know why they never worked out: I was trying too hard. Now, when I counsel young people in their twenties about relationships, I usually say, "Desperate is not attractive, but devotion to God is." I quickly add that devotion to God must not be manipulation to catch someone's eye, but rather a sincere faith in Jesus's challenge to "seek first [God's] kingdom and his righteousness," which comes with the assurance that "all these things will be given to you as well" (Matt 6:33). I tell them that the best way to catch a butterfly is not to chase it at all. Rather, sit down and focus on something important (that is, God), allowing the butterfly to eventually land on your shoulder. And you could say that exactly this happened when I met the woman who would become my wife. Julie lived in Canada. Before our relationship began, I didn't even know that she existed, so I wasn't tempted to chase her or pursue her. This one time in my life, I didn't try to make a relationship with a girl happen. Not only that, but I didn't even try to find her; the Lord simply gave her to me.

My single life was like a roller coaster ride: While I was dating someone, I felt good about myself, but when I wasn't dating, I was in the pits. Once the pit was so deep that I fell into depression. During my senior year of college, I dated a girl for eight months. I thought that she was the one—I was ready to graduate, marry, and get on with life and ministry. But I was in too great a hurry, and she was not ready for marriage. She broke up with me two weeks before I graduated from college, plunging me into a deep depression. It seemed as if all the light and color had left my world. I felt as if my life were overshadowed by huge black storm clouds.

I realize now that my main problem when I was single was that I was looking to girls, rather than to God, for my basic validation as a person. I felt as if I were somehow incomplete if I didn't have a girlfriend, fiancée, or wife. But *one* is a whole number. If you feel like half a person waiting for the second half to come alongside and complete you, then you are going down the wrong road. If you think marriage is the answer to loneliness, then you are being deceived. Believe me: Many married people are still lonely.

Greg Smalley makes this surprising comment in an article on marriage:

One of the greatest truths I've learned about marriage is that I don't need my wife to love me. I know that sounds counterintuitive—maybe even opposite of what you have been taught about relationships. The truth is that your need to be loved has already been satisfied by the right source—your heavenly Father. A spouse will never be the source of love in your life. That is God's role exclusively!

I wish I would have understood and believed the truth of 1 John 3:1 when I was in my early twenties: "How great is the love the Father has lavished on us, that we should be called children of God! And *that is what we are!*" My core identity is Michael, the beloved son of God—regardless of whether I am single or married.

I regret having wasted so much time and energy moping around during the single season of my life. Instead of worrying about getting a date or having a girlfriend, I wish I had spent my energy and time on the affairs of the Lord. To be sure, nothing is wrong with wanting to get married: It is a godly desire. Marriage brings its own benefits and difficulties. I encourage young people who want to get married to honestly cry out to God for a godly life partner. I also challenge them to never lower their standards for whom they marry. The first question I ask when someone tells me that he or she has found someone to date is whether the person he or she has found loves Jesus more than he or she, the person to whom I'm talking. If the person hesitates, I tell him or her that the person in question is not yet dateable material. If that person doesn't love Jesus most of all, then he or she will be tempted to find validation in his or her dating partner. He or she will also be incapable of loving another person in a healthy way. If someone loves Jesus with all his or her heart, then his or her love for a life partner will overflow naturally from that core love.

Tracee, a visiting missionary recruit, once spoke in one of my classes. She was a very attractive woman in her late twenties, and she was on her way to Afghanistan as a missionary. When a student asked her to share about being a single missionary, she replied using a powerful metaphor. Some female friends of hers, she said, had decided to "get out of the race" and sit on the sideline, waiting for a man. But Tracee told the class, "I refuse to get out of the race!" She said that she was resolved to keep running in the direction in which God had called her. If a man were running in the same direction as her and at the same pace, she said, then they would be running beside each other, able to start a friendship that might become a marriage. But she refused to get out of the race and wait for a man.

I wish I had been like Tracee when I was single. My wife, on the other hand, *was* like her. At age 20, Julie made a two-year commitment to go to the DR Congo to do mission work. Her race to the DR Congo took her to the United States for a few days to finalize paperwork with her mission agency. During her few days in the United States, she met me—a man who also wanted to do mission work in the DR Congo, but who had gotten out of the race to wait for a woman. If Julie had not decided to follow the Lord's calling as a single woman, we never would have met.

My best advice for singles is to *stop searching for the right person* and instead *become the right person*—someone who is wholly devoted to the Lord. This will allow the Lord to meet all your needs according to his grace and power, regardless of whether you are single or married. The Apostle Paul was single, and he knew that one of the greatest benefits of the single life was the ability to focus on the Lord's concerns without dividing time and energy between the Lord's concerns and a spouse and children. The single life brings many benefits if you give this season to the Lord in service to his kingdom. Life is brief, and each of its seasons should be lived for the Lord. Don't waste your singleness!

LIFE APPLICATION

1. Make a list of all the benefits of being single. Keep this list where you'll see it often. Add new things to your list as you think of them.

2. Copy the text of Matthew 6:33 on a 3×5 card and place it where you'll see it often as a reminder to seek first the kingdom of God.

3. Reflect on the amount of time and energy you spend thinking about and searching for "the right person." Make some hard decisions that will allow you to put that time to better use, focusing on your devotion to the Lord and his affairs.

CHAPTER 24

THE PARENTING LIFE

Life is too short not to love on your kids

"Children are a reward from him [the Lord]."
Psalm 127:3

At 7:35 p.m. on March 20, 1985, I became a father. As I stood beside my wife in the delivery room of a mission hospital in the DR Congo, four people were in the room: me, Julie, the doctor, and the midwife—and then suddenly there were *five*. Sarah Ann had arrived. No word describes this event better than *miracle*. But only two years later, I found myself in desperate prayer for my feverish Sarah Ann. My precious firstborn child was suffering with malaria, and we couldn't find a way to cure it. Following doctors' advice, we tried different medicines and different doses, taking care to avoid overdosing her. But if the fever went away for a few days, then it came back with a vengeance. Such moments make us realize how vulnerable we are—over how little we have control. Our prayers take on a surprising intensity: "Lord, this is not just anyone; this is *my daughter*!" In a life-threatening moment, the priceless value of a child rushes to the front of our minds and penetrates to the core of our hearts. Then how can we so easily neglect our children and take them for granted in daily living?

I grew up the son of a very busy father, and I remember how deeply the words of Harry Chapin's song "Cat's in the Cradle" pierced my heart the first time I heard them. The song talks about a little boy who tells his father, "I'm gonna be like you, Dad." But the song chronicles the father's neglect of his son. Too busy to play with his son, he keeps making an empty promise: "We'll get together soon and have a good time." But that time never comes. The last verse records how the grown-up boy now has no time for his father— he had indeed grown up to be just like his dad.

As I start writing this chapter, my youngest daughter, Sammy, is midway through her senior year of high school. I have mixed emotions as I contemplate the upcoming empty nest. Part of me looks forward to freedom from parental duties, but part of me is already grieving the loss. When I reflect on our few more months with Sammy at home, life seems to fly by at breakneck speed. Steven Curtis Chapman was inspired to write the song "Cinderella" after being convicted of rushing through bath time with his little daughters. He sensed God telling him to stop and appreciate moments with his kids. His song talks about a father who doesn't want to miss all the moments he has with his daughter, for she will soon grow up and be gone. The song refers to the clock striking midnight in the Cinderella Story when all of a sudden Cinderella is gone. The message of his own song became more personal and powerful for Steven when, soon after he wrote it, his 5-year-old girl was killed in a tragic accident in the driveway of their home.

Children can die from many causes. My friend Jeff Butler worked in a risky occupation, serving as a pilot for a relief and development agency in Kenya. My heart broke when I heard that Jeff had been shot by bandits in a village near the Somalia border. Single and only 27 years old, Jeff was doing what he wanted to do, but that didn't lessen his parents' pain at having to say goodbye so soon. My daughter-in-law, Chelsea, lost her little brother to heart complications when he was only 7 months old. Whether death comes at 27 years or 7 months, the death of a child before a parent seems so very unnatural. I heard Bob Szoke say to someone in the funeral visitation line how it didn't seem right to him that Steve had died before he himself had. During his fight with cancer, Steve himself acknowledged that his mother and father wished that they, instead of Steve, had been the ones diagnosed with cancer.

And, of course, parents sometimes also die—as it seems—before their time. My friend Ashley lost her father when she was a young girl. My good friend David lost his father, who, seemingly in good health in his early sixties, went to be with the Lord while sitting at home in his easy chair. A few years ago, I shared a serious conversation with one of my students about her father, who was in his fifties and in bad health; she was in her early twenties and was worried that he would not live until she got married. Our conversation took place in April, and her father died that July. We don't know when our kids will die, nor do we know when we ourselves will die—and life is way too short to live with regret. When my parents were in their late seventies, my mother was not in good health. After Dad told me how Mom "brightens up" whenever she gets a call from one of her kids, I accepted his challenge to call her regularly. I tried to call her every weekend, just to see how she was doing. I reasoned that if I were to die before my mother did, I wanted her to be able to remember her last conversation with me; and if my mother died before I did, I wanted to remember how I ended our most recent conversation with "I love you, Mom!" As it turned out, my mother died at the age of 81 from a sudden heart attack unable to speak to her children before she died. Remembering that I concluded my last phone conversation a few days earlier with her using the words, "I love you mom!" indeed gave me comfort.

When my daughter Sammy was a senior in High School, I asked her how I could pray for her for an entire year. She asked me to pray that she would improve her relationship with God. I realized that I needed to be more intentional in my spiritual leadership in her life: I had only one more year with her at home. You can help your kids with lots of things, from teaching them to tie their shoes to helping them learn to drive. But the most important thing you can do is help them improve their relationship with God. The goal of parenting is not to raise an "independent" person who can stand on his or her own, with no need for anyone else. Neither is it to raise a "dependent" person who will always need his or her parents. Rather, the purpose of parenting is to *transfer the object of your children's dependence* from you to God. Because life is so brief, parents must focus on things that have eternal value.

I love praying for my kids. I gained insight into the importance of parental prayer for children from the Old Testament book of Job. Job 1:3 calls Job "the greatest man among all the people of the East," and the following verses describe his regular custom of offering a burned offering to God on behalf of each of his ten children. Job interceded for his children on a regular basis, his main concern their passion for God and the purity of their lives. And rightly so, for Job personally experienced the brevity and fragility of life when he lost all his children in a single catastrophe.

For the past several years, I have prayed over my children every morning. My prayers center on the following items for each of my children:

- Passion (for God above all else)
- Protection (from physical and emotional harm and from the lies of the enemy)
- Purity (ethical, moral, sexual)
- Presence (experiencing the loving presence of the Lord)
- Power (experiencing the daily strength of the Lord)
- Partner (loving and respecting his or her marriage partner, or prayer for a future marriage partner)
- Purpose (knowing his or her calling in life)
- Peace (experiencing the peace of God in their heart)

Bruce, a friend of mine, always ends conversations with his kids, whether over the telephone or in person, with the words "I love you." Should he ever die quickly or unexpectedly, without the chance to speak to his kids, he wants the last words they remember to be "I love you"—for he doesn't want his kids to ever doubt his love. None of us knows how long we will have our kids; life is way too short to neglect the opportunity to embrace and enjoy them every day the Lord gives you with them.

LIFE APPLICATION

1. Do you see your children as a *temporary gift* to you—on loan from God? Ask God to give you this perspective. Pray over your children every day, as Job did. Use photos or other reminders to trigger your prayers.

2. Have you asked your children to let you know when they need more of your time and attention? If not, regularly ask them whether they do.

3. Do you regularly express your love for your children before leaving their presence (including in telephone and Internet communications)? Check in weekly, biweekly, or monthly (by email or phone, if necessary) with both your parents and your kids.

CHAPTER 25

THE OTHER-FOCUSED LIFE

Life is too short to focus on yourself

"Do not think of yourself more highly than you ought,
but rather think of yourself with sober judgment, in
accordance with the measure of faith God has given you."
Romans 12:3

"Do nothing out of selfish ambition or vain conceit, but in humility
consider others better than yourselves. Each of you should look not
only to your own interests, but also to the interests of others."
Philippians 2:3–4

We are all incredibly self-focused, selfish people, and only through great intentional effort will we become other-focused people. We must be so overwhelmed by the love of God for us that we look for validation only from God. Accepting and believing in God's great love for us will free us to be other-focused people. We will be motivated to love others purely, not with an eye to what they can give us in return. The

Apostle Paul was clear about what motivated him. In 2 Corinthians 5:14, he says, "For Christ's love compels us, because we are convinced that one died for all." Verse 15 shows us how this connects with becoming "other-focused": "And he died for all, that those who live *should no longer live for themselves* but for him who died for them and was raised again."

When we become amazed by God's love for us, we have no problem giving our lives in service to him by focusing on others and serving them. Paul never forgot the amazing love and grace that God poured out in his own life. In 1 Timothy 1:14–15, we see that Paul never took God's grace to him for granted:

The grace of our Lord was poured out on me abundantly, along with the faith and love that are in Christ Jesus. Here is a trustworthy saying that deserves full acceptance: Christ Jesus came into the world to save sinners—of whom I am the worst.

Many years ago I heard a preacher illustrate God's love and grace in a way I have never forgotten. He talked about how everyone loves to hold and cuddle a baby who is happy and smells good. But imagine the baby in another situation, having just spit up all over itself, its diaper oozing at the edges. No one wants to hold and cuddle such a baby! The preacher asked us to picture such a baby in the middle of the floor, left in all its mess, utterly helpless to clean itself up. But, he said, Romans 5:6–8 tells us that at this exact moment, God reached down to pick us up:

You see, at just the right time, when we were still powerless, Christ died for the ungodly. Very rarely will anyone die for a righteous man, though for a good man someone might possibly dare to die. But God demonstrates his own love for us in this: While we were still sinners, Christ died for us.

When you and I realize the depth of God's love for us, we are freed to love others. Jesus told us to love our neighbors as we love ourselves. The key to loving others is believing that we are loved deeply by God. We aren't capable of becoming other-focused people until we love ourselves first. Doing so is not selfishness or pride: It is simply believing the truth of God's love for us. Other-focused people are humble, not proud. One of the foundational secrets to having humility is knowing that you are loved by God. C. S. Lewis, speaking of humility in *Mere Christianity*, says that when you meet a truly humble man, you probably wouldn't think him humble—you would simply enjoy being in his presence. He would be so comfortable being himself that he would not focus on himself at all—he would be focused on others and on God. I have spent much of my life focused on what other people thought of me. In a social situation, I have often focused on what others were thinking about me, wondering particularly whether they liked me. When you are self-conscious, preoccupied with what others are thinking about you, you have no time or energy to focus on them. When you know that you are loved by God at the core of your being, you don't have to search for love and affirmation from people around you—and this frees you to focus on others, not yourself.

When my daughter Sarah was standing in the bathroom in a fancy dress, fixing her hair for prom, I teased her about all the self-conscious young men and women who would be at prom that night. I asked her whether she realized that every person at the prom would be focusing on himself or herself, each one asking the same question: *How do I look to the other people here?* I remarked on how amusing it would be watching the prom from God's perspective, seeing every person asking the same self-focused question and no one actually focusing on how anyone *else* looked. Sarah, who didn't appreciate my insightful reflections, shooed me out of the bathroom.

Indeed, focusing on yourself isn't difficult. This past year, I took part in a Lenten service held forty days before Easter. In the past, I had never given up anything for Lent, but I decided to give it a try. After trying to think about something I wanted to stop doing, I decided not to talk about myself unless in answer to someone else's question. I tried hard to keep this vow for the forty days leading up to Easter—and I found out just how difficult not focusing on oneself can be.

Other-focused people are great listeners. When we listen, we can be selective, attentive, or empathic. When we listen selectively, we focus only partially on others, hearing only part of what they say—often only the parts we want to hear. When we listen attentively, we pay attention to the other person and probably will remember what he or she said to us. But a deeper level still is empathic listening—listening with the intent to truly understand the other person and try to feel what he or she is feeling. With this kind of listening, you listen with your eyes, mind, and heart—not just your ears. You are trying to read the other person's body language and nonverbal signals, empathizing with his or her feelings. Other-focused people do more listening than talking. Perhaps, as the saying goes, the reason why God created us with two ears and one mouth was to remind us to listen twice as much as we speak.

Other-focused people are great learners. When I first started teaching at Lincoln Christian University, the name of the department in which I taught was "World Missions." Missions is a good word, but many see it as having a one-way focus: *I am on a mission to tell you something.* Much of the mission work done by Western missionaries in the last two centuries has involved cultural imperialism, with the gospel often presented in such a way as to expect converts to accept Christ and Western "civilized" culture simultaneously. So we decided to change the name of our department from "World Missions" to "Intercultural Studies." We still understood that we had a core gospel message we needed to share—the message of reconciliation (2 Cor 5:18–20)—but we also knew we had much to learn from other people about their own cultures and beliefs. Indeed, we could never share an appropriately contextualized gospel message that would be received and understood as good news until we took the time to learn the language and culture of others. The department title "Intercultural Studies" is humbler and wiser: It is other-focused.

The world is becoming internationalized today, especially in urban areas. And we have much to learn from other cultures. Every culture has both good and bad elements, every culture its own blind spots. When we develop intercultural relationships, we can help each other see our own cultural blind spots. I believe in absolute truth, but because of my cultural filters, I cannot absolutely apprehend it but only partially grasp it. That is why relationships with Christian brothers and sisters who are from other cultures are so important. They can help us correct inadequacies in our own theology, and we can help them correct theirs.

The world has come to America, with more than 900,000 international students studying in the United States every year. How sad it is that many Americans don't even notice. Most of these students want to make American friends, but most will never be invited into an American home. The majority of these students come from unreached areas of the world, and most have never heard the good news of Jesus clearly presented. When they return to their home countries after graduation, most of these students will have positions of influence in politics, education, and business. I cannot think of a more strategic focus for intercultural ministry today. But we need other-focused Christians in America to notice. And so I encourage the students on our campus to get to know as many international students as possible during their years in university. I tell them that each international student is a walking cultural library. What a shame it would be to spend four years on the same campus with an international student and never take the opportunity to tap into the wisdom of that student's culture. Because every human being from every culture bears the image of God (Gen 1:27), we can learn something about God from any person we meet—if we are other-focused.

When my father hosted a Congolese church leader in America for a short visit, they traveled to many different churches across the Midwest. Near the end of the leader's visit, he sadly said to my father, "Everywhere we have gone, people have showed me things and have told me much about America. But could you have someone ask me about my country?" Life is too short to focus only on ourselves.

LIFE APPLICATION

1. What is your attitude toward other people? Do you notice others around you? Do you see people from other cultures?

2. What reminders can you put in your life to help you quit focusing on yourself and to make you a better listener to—and learner of—others? Adopt a general rule of listening twice as much as you speak. Come up with a few open-ended questions to ask people as a way of encouraging them to share about their lives.

3. In what ways are you tempted to think of yourself as being better than others? Compose a prayer that you can pray daily to help you remove your focus from yourself. Consider making a vow to not initiate talk about yourself for a season.

CHAPTER 26

THE DIBS LIFE

Life is too short to snub people who have been created in God's image

> *"So God created man in his own image, in the image of God he created him; male and female he created them."*
> **Genesis 1:27**

> *"There simply are no neutral human encounters."*
> **Duane Elmer**

I gnoring the people around us every day is easy to do. We walk by so many people whom we don't even see, let alone acknowledge—they just seem like part of the scenery. Can you imagine having this embarrassing conversation with another human being, created in the image of God, when you get to heaven?

> You: "Hi! What's your name? I don't think I've met you before."
>
> Person: "I know who *you* are. I bagged your groceries (or fixed your car, cut your hair, or prepared your coffee) for years when we were on Earth."

C. S. Lewis wrote that we nudge people toward one of two destinies by how we treat them. In his book, *The Weight of Glory*, he explains how every contact with another human has a way of helping that person to one of two destinies:

There are no ordinary people. You have never talked to a mere mortal ... It is immortals whom we joke with, work with, marry, snub and exploit—immortal horrors or everlasting splendors ... Our interactions with people are helping to nudge them toward one destiny or another ... Next to the blessed sacrament itself—your neighbor is the holiest object presented to your senses. (Lewis, 1949, 19)

During my doctoral studies, I encountered attribution theory, which deals with the qualities that we attribute to people either before we actually meet them or in the first moments after meeting them. Many times, this means negative attribution when we see something we don't like—tattoos, long hair, dirty clothes, baggy jeans, or so forth. Even though my professor expressed dislike for the constant invention of new sociological terms, I decided to create one of my own: *prior value placement*.

Using this term, I refer to the human ability to consciously place a positive value on another person before even making contact with him or her. And we can certainly also do this in our first few seconds/minutes of interacting for the first time with another human being. I believe that this principle is powerful enough to solve difficult problems such as ethnocentrism, prejudice, and racism. It is based on the foundational principle found in Genesis 1: "So God created man *in his own image*, in the image of God he created him; male and female he created them" (Gen 1:27).

This one short verse holds the key for horizontal human relationship problems, speaking of the inherent value and worth of every human being who will ever exist. How powerful to think that each human is a unique image-bearer of God! Indeed, humans are sacred, for we are intrinsically connected to the divine through creation. This single thought can change how we view—and how we treat—each person we meet in this life.

Another verse, this one from Revelation, the last book in the Bible, can change our attitude about people's value as well. John writes in Revelation:

After this I looked and there before me was a great multitude that no one could count, from every nation, tribe, people and language, standing before the throne and in front of the Lamb. They were wearing white robes and were holding palm branches in their hands. And they cried out in a loud voice: "Salvation belongs to our God, who sits on the throne, and to the Lamb." (Rev 7:9–10)

If we can wrap our minds around the concluding big picture of history presented to us in this passage, we will change how we think about people. Because the citizenship of heaven will be made up of people from every ethnic and language group on the face of the Earth, there is no place for ignoring or snubbing anyone.

Asking the Lord to change your perspective on the essential value of a person can change how you look at each person you meet on planet Earth, from now until the day you die. Duane Elmer, in his book *Cross-Cultural Servanthood*, tells how back in the mid-1990s, he and his wife spent some late nights on the streets of Chicago, learning how to minister to people. One night, walking with an experienced street minister, Elmer noticed a woman at the next corner:

She was scantily clad. I turned to him and said in a voice the lady would not hear, "Is she a prostitute?" He paused; I remember thinking, *Why the pause? It's obvious.* Then he said firmly, "No! That's not a prostitute. That's a person … in prostitution." His profound statement affects me to this day. When I saw this woman, I saw a prostitute. When Mark saw her, he saw a human being. (Elmer, 2006, 64)

Our tendency to categorize people is a natural one, and doing so isn't wrong—so long as the first category in which we place people is *human, created in the image of God.* I like to invent mental "triggers" to help me remember important things. Not too long ago I came up with a trigger word to help me value all people: the acronym DIBs, short for "divine image-bearers." We all know what the word *dibs* means: It signifies a prior claim. I have decided to intentionally use this acronym as a mental trigger whenever I see someone—in my mind I try to say, "He's (or she's) got dibs!" In other words, he or she has a prior claim to value simply by bearing the image of God. This mental trigger has helped me immensely, especially when encountering people who could easily otherwise become part of the scenery, such as cashiers, servers, and store clerks. Thinking in terms of DIBs is also very helpful when I first meet someone to whom I'm tempted to attribute negative traits.

How quickly we make decisions about the worth of people we meet! Based on a visual scan, we can categorize a person in mere seconds, deciding whether we want to get to know him or her or even speak to him or her at all. I'm frightened by realizing that I can decide whether a person I meet is "worthy of a relationship with me" based on so little information. Such a decision is a form of prejudice. Indeed, *prejudice* means "pre-judging"—making a judgment without the benefit of all the facts. If we are not careful, prejudice will become our natural, daily mode of operation with people. We must intentionally reprogram our minds with the truth of Genesis 1:27: *Every person I meet is created in the image of God.* And if Genesis 1:27 is true, then I am seeing the image of God in every person I meet in my life—even nonbelievers and adherents of other religions. I might even learn something about God from the people I meet. Moreover, if Genesis 1:27 is true, then there are no "common people," no "little people," no "dirty people," and no "inferior people." Life is too short to ignore the value of people. This simple concept can change the world—and it might save you from some embarrassing conversations in heaven, too!

LIFE APPLICATION

1. What people do you regularly ignore and snub, treating as if they are part of the background scenery? List these people, but don't stop at that—make a point of learning their names and beginning meaningful conversations with them.

2. Do some no-holds-barred self-examination. Conduct a brutally honest internal assessment to identify those to whom you are tempted to feel superior. Honestly reflect on some of the "lower values" you ascribe to people because of external things such as clothing, tattoos, or demeanor.

3. Write "DIBs" on something that you will see every day to remind you that every person you meet is a divine image-bearer. Get into the habit of seeing and speaking a word of encouragement to the "service sector" people with whom you interact during a normal day or week (at gas stations, stores, tollbooths, and the like).

CHAPTER 27

THE INTERGENERATIONAL LIFE

Life is too short to spend it only with people your own age

> *"We will tell the next generation the praiseworthy deeds*
> *of the Lord, his power, and the wonders he has done."*
> **Psalm 78:4**

> *"One generation will commend your works*
> *to another; they will tell of your mighty acts."*
> **Psalm 145:4**

Intergenerational relationships can be some of the most rewarding in life, but crossing the generation gap takes courage. I deal with this divide every time I walk into the cafeteria of the university where I teach. In that moment, I have to decide whether to sit with other faculty and staff—which is far more comfortable, not least because we have many things in common—or to sit with students instead. I don't remember ever being turned down by a student when asking whether I could sit with him or her during lunch, but still I fear being rejected. I fear invading students' space, worrying that they really don't want to be seen with me or to talk to me in a social setting. In the classroom, I have the power to ask questions and initiate discussions. But in the cafeteria, I'm just another hungry person looking for a place to sit and eat lunch.

My struggle over where to sit in the cafeteria has decreased over the years. I no longer believe the lies Satan has whispered to me, telling me that students don't really like professors or that students don't want to spend time with people who are older than they. I have learned that students love to have relationships with people who are older than they—and that they are just as scared as I am to cross the generational gap. I have had too many good results from my lunches with students over the years to believe Satan's lies any longer. Some students have joined my major because I took the time to talk to them at lunch; others have come to me for counsel because I took the time to learn their name over lunch and asked how they were doing.

God loves people of all generations. The Bible encourages Christians to pass on the praises and teachings of God to every new generation (Deut 6:1–9, Ps 78:3–6). Jesus stood up and advocated for the youngest generation, which was being pushed aside in his days (Mark 10:13–16). On the birthday of the Church, Peter quoted the prophet Joel, who spoke about God pouring out his Spirit during the last days so that "sons and daughters will prophesy," young men would "see visions," and old men would "dream dreams" (Acts 2:17). The Apostle Paul told a young man named Timothy to not let people look down on him because he was young (1 Tim 4:12). God calls himself a "father to the fatherless," saying that his job is setting the "lonely in families" (Ps 68:5–6). The younger generation is close to God's heart, but unfortunately, its members are not always a priority among older members of the Church. Yet the Church is only one generation from extinction—a constant reminder for all Christians. Satan desires to bring discord and division into the Church, and intergenerational relationships provide the perfect place for him to breed neglect and division.

Young people can tell whether an older person truly likes them. They know instinctively whether they are included as "part of the family." Some church leaders who fear change have felt threatened by youth whom they suspect want to "take their position" in leadership. Future young leaders often hear older leaders in the Church saying, "Sit here under my authority—and wait!" True spiritual fathers and mothers, on the other hand, make space for their spiritual sons and daughters, encouraging them to succeed. True intergenerational leadership development in the Church must go deeper than merely the training and development of replacements—it must include affectionate, emotional bonding that comes with the idea of being a spiritual intergenerational family.

God can heal intergenerational wounds if a new generation of youth can be loved, taught, and empowered to follow Jesus. In the New Testament, we see the Apostle Paul spiritually adopting and parenting young Timothy and young Onesimus, helping them become leaders and countercultural forces in the first century. The world needs more fathers and mothers in Christ who will spiritually adopt the young people in their churches, helping them become empowered leaders for the church of the twenty-first century. Today's youth cry out for spiritual parents. Indeed, solving intergenerational issues and building strong intergenerational relationships may be one of the most important tasks the Church faces.

Younger and older generations in the Church might well have many good ideas for intergenerational interaction, but what seems to be lacking is intent leading to action. Just as in the cafeteria, I think both sides are intimidated by the other, each waiting for the other side to take the first step.

With multiple different generational sub-cultures existing within our culture, walls of separation arise easily, whether intentionally or through neglect. Bridging generational cultures will take cross-cultural skills, such as observation, asking questions, listening, language-learning, and culture-learning. Cross-generational "missionaries" will need to remember that words and actions are defined as respectful and loving according to the perception of the receiving generation. Older and younger generations must make every effort to bring down the intergenerational walls that have been erected in the Church, without regard to who takes the first step—perhaps even both at the same time!

In Matthew 21, Jesus reminded the Jewish leaders that God had ordained praise from children and infants (Matt 21:14–16), and by extension this includes youth as well. The youth in our churches have been ordained by God to worship him—and to become leaders in the Church. Older generations must come to grips with this truth for the Church to continue and prosper. We must look to Scripture for biblical models of intergenerational relationships. The importance of bridging generation gaps is exemplified in our Lord. The gospels depict Jesus as an advocate for children and youth, a role that was shocking in a culture that placed little value on children. Jesus said, "Whoever welcomes a little child like this in my name welcomes me," and he warned, "If anyone causes one of these little ones who believe in me to sin, it would be better for him to have a large millstone hung around his neck and to be drowned in the depths of the sea" (Matt 18:5–6). Jesus emphasized God's unwillingness "that any of these little ones should be lost" (Matt 18:14).

The Old Testament records healthy intergenerational relationships and leadership transition models in the stories of Moses and Joshua and of Elijah and Elisha. The Old Testament also includes examples of what happens when one generation does not listen to another, as when Solomon's son Rehoboam rejected the good advice of the elders for the bad advice of the young men with whom he had grown up, a decision that ultimately divided the kingdom of Israel (1 Kings 12). God's perspective on children and youth is seen in his description of himself as a "father to the fatherless" (Ps 68:5). God expects older leaders to "bear fruit in old age" (Ps 92:14) and expects one generation to commend the works of the Lord to another generation (Ps 145:4).

We must continue to find ways to restore the broken connections between the generations. Both younger and older generations need each other, and the world needs them both. Negative stereotypes exist in both younger and older generations, but both have many positives to give the other. Two Congolese sayings, spoken side by side, can help bridge the generational divide. When an older person in the DR Congo desires to put young people "in their place," he or she might be heard to say, "I saw the sun before you did"; but a young person might counter with another local saying: "A little boy can play the drum, and the elderly will dance to it."

God wants to purify his Church of things such as intergenerational conflict, opening the way for him to use the Church as a tool for revival and healing. Our lives are short; we must not miss our window of opportunity. Jesus said that "every teacher of the law who has been instructed about the kingdom of heaven is like the owner of a house who brings out of his storeroom *new* treasures as well as *old*" (Matt 13:52). Both the younger and older generations in the Church have treasures to share, but they need a relationship of trust between them before they can appreciate the value of each other's treasures. Life is too short not to appreciate and use all the treasures God has given to the different generations in the Church.

LIFE APPLICATION

1. What fears or anxieties do you have about generations older or younger than yours?
2. How can you purposefully speak to someone who is of a younger or older generation in your church or at your workplace?
3. Name three younger or older people for whom you can begin to pray daily.

CHAPTER 28

THE UNPREJUDICED LIFE

Life is too short to pre-judge people

> *"There is neither Jew nor Greek, slave nor free,*
> *male nor female, for you are all one in Christ Jesus."*
> **Galatians 3:28**

> *"After this I looked and there before me was a great multitude*
> *that no one could count, from every nation, tribe, people and*
> *language, standing before the throne and in front of the Lamb.*
> *They were wearing white robes and were holding palm branches*
> *in their hands. And they cried out in a loud voice: 'Salvation*
> *belongs to our God, who sits on the throne, and to the Lamb'"*
> **Rev 7:9–10**

I f you don't like people from other "races" or ethnic groups, you probably won't enjoy heaven. Wrapping our minds around the big picture of history presented to us in Revelation 7 will affect how we think about all people. Since the membership of heaven will be made up of people from every ethnic and language group on Earth, God's kingdom has no place for ethnocentrism, racism, or prejudice. Prejudice simply means to "pre-judge" someone—that is, judging without the benefit of all the facts about him or her, which no human will ever have. Only God is qualified to judge people, because he does know all the facts.

Everyone seems to have someone, perhaps some group of people, on whom he or she looks down or whom he or she considers inferior. And the Church has been one of the worst culprits when it comes to race and class differences. In his book *Divided by Faith*, Michael Emerson asks a glaring question: "Why are the members of more than 90 percent of all religious congregations in America still composed almost entirely of one race—even where the general population is racially diverse?" He goes on to ask other difficult questions:

What deeply held, often unconscious, notions about each other underlie our choices of the people with whom we form meaningful relationships? What attitudes about people of another race do we reveal in our most private moments—often in the form of racial jokes?

Since childhood, I have had a nagging prejudice against Polish people. And I didn't even know any Polish people growing up! The source of my prejudice was Polack jokes—jokes about Polish people. In every joke I heard, a Polish person was the butt of the joke, portrayed as incredibly stupid. A few years ago, I took some university students on a short-term missions trip to Poland. On our trip, I met Polish people who were some of the most intelligent, godly, caring people I have ever known. One day, I felt convicted to confess my long-standing internal prejudice to a Polish brother in Christ named George. He graciously forgave me and prayed for me. Praise God— these negative thoughts and feelings of prejudice are now gone from my life forever! Every time I hear of Polish people or Poland now, my first thoughts are always very positive.

This incident caused me to reflect on the origins of prejudice and racism. In this case, it came from sheer ignorance—having never actually known any

Polish people, I was responding to hearsay. Polack jokes began during World War II and were exacerbated by the arrival of Polish immigrants in America, when those seeing themselves as "real Americans" reacted to the actions of strangers and newcomers. Of course people coming from another culture do and say things that seem stupid—they don't know how the new culture works! I can just imagine the things said about the "stupid foreigner" when I first arrived as a missionary in the DR Congo.

Another prejudicial stereotype with which I grew up, thanks to Cold War propaganda, vilified Russian people. I would love to visit Russia someday to get to know some real Russian people, changing the negative perceptions of them that have been in my mind since childhood. There is something powerful about investing in a one-on-one relationship with someone who is different from you, especially someone who belongs to a group of people against whom you have harbored negative feelings. I remember the simple, yet profound challenge from a Promise Keepers conference I attended in the 1990s. The 50,000 men in that Indianapolis stadium were challenged to find a man from another ethnic group and to start an intentional friendship—for walls of prejudice and racism can come down *one person at a time*. Only think what could happen between Hutus and Tutsis in Rwanda, Jews and Muslims in the Middle East, or Democrats and Republicans in America.

A few years ago, I took a class on ethnicity at Trinity International University in which I realized that the conception of race as a biological or physical reality that can be used to demonstrate how one group of people is superior to another is actually a 400-year-old lie based on no credible evidence—nothing! And twisted theology was used to support this lie. For example, some have spoken of the "curse of Ham" as being somehow connected to the black race. But the phrase *curse of Ham* is not found in the Bible, which speaks rather of the curse of Canaan, Ham's son—and Canaan became the father of people who live in the Middle East, not in Africa! Moreover, science has helped expose the lie of race superiority: The Human

Genome Project has shown that humans are overwhelmingly similar in their genetic makeup.

When I was listening to a radio call-in program while driving across Missouri, a woman called to complain that her daughter, who was white, wanted to date an African American boy. The mother asked for scriptural support for a prohibition on interracial dating. She remembered hearing about a Bible verse that warned against being "unequally yoked" and wanted to know where she could find it. The radio host told the woman that the phrase she was thinking about was from 2 Corinthians 6:14–18 but explained that the phrase was referring to a Christian marrying a non-Christian—that it had nothing to do with different races. Then he said something that I have never forgotten: "Ma'am, you need to know that there is actually only one race mentioned in the Bible, and that is the human race!"

I have reflected on that statement many times. What if we really believed that there was only one race—the human race? It would change so many things. I would love to mature, by God's grace, to the point of laying down the oppressive burden of negatively judging other people according to skin color, culture, or class. Indeed, Henri Nouwen in his book *Here and Now* writes about a time in his life when he felt free from this bondage:

It felt as if a heavy burden had been taken away from me. At those moments I experienced an immense love for everyone I met, heard about, or read about. A deep solidarity with all people and a deep desire to love them broke down all my inner walls and made my heart as wide as the universe … I was so full of God's goodness wherever I went, even behind the facades of violence, destruction and crime. I had to restrain myself from embracing the women and men who sold me groceries, flowers, and a new suit. They all seemed like saints to me! (Nouwen, 1994, 69-70)

I used to struggle with what to do when I came across a homeless person on the sidewalk, thinking *What should I do? What should I say?* Then Don, a friend of mine, told me, "Mike, why don't you just treat them like an ordinary person? Look them in the eye, and talk to them normally?" His advice was helpful and profound. Life is too short not to treat every person I meet as a fellow member of the human race—a divine image-bearer of God. Since we will be hanging out for all eternity with people from every ethnic group and social class, shouldn't we get to know as many different people as we can during our short time on Earth?

LIFE APPLICATION

1. Be brutally honest with yourself. Against what groups, nationalities, or classes of people have you felt negative prejudice?
2. Take the Promise Keepers challenge: Find a way to purposefully begin a friendship with someone from a different ethnic group.
3. The next time you see a homeless person on the street, don't ignore or avoid him or her. Walk up and look him or her in the face, asking his or her name and introducing yourself. Talk to that person just as you would any other person, treating him or her with dignity for being a member of your race—the human race.

CHAPTER 29

THE ADVOCATING LIFE

Life is too short not to stick your neck out for someone

"Speak up for those who cannot speak for themselves."
Proverbs 31:8

*"The only thing necessary for the triumph
of evil is for good men to do nothing."*
Edmund Burke

C an you imagine God asking you in heaven why you didn't stick up for someone who needed help during your life on Earth? The first time I remembering needing to stick up for someone came when I was attending junior high in Potomac, Illinois. While waiting for the school bus, some kids started picking on my younger brother, Stevie. Stevie had experienced brain damage at birth and attended special education classes in school. His speech has never been very clear, and as a child he had trouble controlling his saliva glands, which meant that his shirts usually had a wet spot in front. And so the kids started calling Stevie "retarded"; someone called him a "slobber-box." An anger rose inside me that surprised me—I was ready to fight them all.

When the other kids saw my clenched fists and the fire in my eyes, they backed off, stopping their teasing and name-calling. After cooling down, I pondered the source of my surprising reaction. Partly, I was surprised because *I liked to pick on Stevie, too*—when we were at home. Stevie was very stubborn, and we got in lots of fights together. But when someone else was picking on him, I was ready to fight for him.

I love movies in which a hero sticks up for someone who has no power or who is without a voice. In the amazing movie *42*, for example, I can't get enough of Branch Rickey sticking up for Jackie Robinson. In my favorite scene, Peewee Reese, whose family and friends were sitting in the stands that day, put his arm around Jackie. Several were very upset that a "Negro" was trying to play professional baseball with white men, but the movie showed how Reese's friendly attitude toward Jackie influenced a small boy in the stands, even though he was surrounded by racist people.

When I became a youth minister, someone from the Illinois Department of Children and Family Services approached me about becoming an "advocate." At first I didn't really know what the word entailed, but now I love it: It simply means someone who sticks up for someone else. In French, defense attorneys are called advocates. I agreed to become an advocate for a small 10-year-old boy named Clarence. In his short life, he had already experienced much physical, sexual, and emotional abuse, and he had no positive male role model. I did my best to love and encourage Clarence, knowing that he was fighting an uphill battle in life. Sometimes I thought *At least Clarence has one person in his life who is trying to help him rather than abuse him.*

I played the same role of advocate when I arrived in the DR Congo to serve as a youth minister. The children and youth of the DR Congo were considered second-class citizens, having no voice of influence in their culture. The very idea of youth ministry was a foreign concept to the Congolese church. No one had ever heard of such a thing. I was there to advocate—to raise a flag for the importance of young people and wave it.

One of my favorite scenes in Jesus's life is found in Mark 10. When the disciples tried to shoo away some kids, Jesus got very angry. In fact, Jesus went ballistic. He stood up for the children, demanding that the disciples let them come to him. He took the children in his arms and blessed them before sending them away. Similarly, the Apostle Paul was an advocate for a young runaway slave named Onesimus, a good parallel for many at-risk teens of today.

The word *compassion* means "suffering with" or "suffering alongside." Many are suffering today who have no voice of influence—nor anyone advocating for them. If you are looking for voiceless people, simply look to the margins of society. Look at both ends of the age range—unborn children, still in the womb, and older people in nursing homes. Look at children who live in abusive situations, struggling single mothers, or immigrants who don't speak English. Scripture describes God as a defender of widows and children and aliens—those who are marginalized, having no voice. Life is too short not to speak out on someone else's behalf. Wouldn't you like to look back on your life, remembering voiceless people whom you helped speak? Won't it be great to meet people in heaven someday who thank you for speaking up for them when you could have walked away instead?

God has brought an amazing young Congolese man into my life whose name is Tresor. Tresor simply wants to help those in society who have no voice. Tresor has reached out to former child soldiers, street kids, and rape survivors in the DR Congo. Thanks to his encouragement, I have been able to join him in reaching out to about twenty young girls who were kidnapped and raped during fighting in the DR Congo. These girls need advocates badly, for many have been rejected by their own families after escaping their captors and returning to their original homes.

On a trip to the DR Congo, I was asked to hold a one-day teaching seminar for these girls, who had been abducted and raped multiple times by

Hutu extremists hiding out in the forests of eastern Congo. I was humbled trying to think of a way to help these girls who had been hurt so deeply. But then I remembered an illustration used by a youth minister in the United States to speak to youth about their value. I started by holding up a $100 bill—they understood the value of American currency, which is frequently used in their country. I asked, "Does anyone want this $100 bill?" Everyone's hand shot up immediately. Then I surprised them by crumpling the bill in my hands, then slowly unrolling it. I asked, "Who wants it now?" Everyone's hand stayed up. Then I threw the bill down and ground it into the dirt with my foot. I spit on it. When I picked up the bill, held it before the group a third time, and asked whether anyone still wanted it, *everyone* still wanted it. Then I asked the girls: Why did they still want a bill that had been abused in so many ways? Because the bill had intrinsic value, holding its worth no matter what was done to its exterior. The girls got the point. They were still valuable, beloved daughters of God, no matter what had been done to them.

Sometimes we are overwhelmed by the size of our task and the sheer amount of people needing advocates. As Mother Teresa said, "we cannot all do great things, but we can all do small things with great love." Tresor has adopted the phrase "small things; great love" as a motto for Mwangaza (Swahili for "shining/dawning light"), a nonprofit organization he started in the DR Congo.

Several years ago, my mother made me a birthday card reading "The first great rule in life is *to put up with things*; the second is *to refuse to put up with things*; and the third, and hardest, is to be able to distinguish between the first two." Life is too short to put up with things that should not be put up with! I pray that God makes me sick and troubled enough over injustice to act. Justice is not about pity, nor about having feelings of sympathy. Justice is about biblical compassion—when something touches you at the core of your being and causes you to act.

In summer 2008, I returned to Africa after a fifteen-year absence. Flying over Darfur (western Sudan) at 37,000 feet, I reflected on what I was doing as a parable for our times. Horrible things were happening below me, but I didn't see them, because I was flying at 37,000 feet. By flying over in a plane, I was living on a different plain. Hurting people are all around us, in our town and across the sea. But do we see them? Do we hear them? Will we take up the role of advocate for them? Life is too short not to stick your neck out for someone else who needs your help.

LIFE APPLICATION

1. The Bible calls us to hate evil. How can you keep your "hatred for injustice" alive?

2. Ask God to make you sick and troubled enough about an injustice that you move from pity to compassion, causing you to act.

3. What people live near you who don't have influential voices? What people in other nations don't have voices, for whom you can be an advocate?

CHAPTER 30

THE ENCOURAGING-WORD LIFE

Life is too short not to speak life

"An anxious heart weighs a man down, but a kind word cheers him up."
Proverbs 12:25

*"Our chief want is someone who will
inspire us to be what we know we could be."*
Ralph Waldo Emerson

I received a shocking phone call from an old friend—I'll call him "Doug"—one Christmas. I had not talked to Doug since junior high school, and he was drunk, depressed, and suicidal. He had found my contact information using the Internet and had decided to reach out to his old friend Mike to see whether I had any words of encouragement for him before he took his life. After much conversation, urgent prayer, pleading, and encouragement, Doug got rid of his handgun. He later told me that he threw it into the middle of the pond at a golf course near his house. After sobering up, he flew to spend Christmas with his parents in another state. You never know when someone needs to hear a word of encouragement—a word that may end up saving his or her life.

Discouragement and discouraging words have been around a long time, ever since Eden. I believe that discouragement is one of Satan's most effective weapons. My seminary professor told our class about receiving a special plaque as a gift when he was a missionary in Africa. It read: "I steadfastly refuse to gratify the devil by becoming discouraged!" Authentic spiritual warfare lies behind that sentence. I now have a yellow sticky note on the bulletin board in my office bearing those same words; I am looking at it as I type this. Satan will always find ways to discourage us, so we need people in our life who can counter his words of death by speaking words of life to us. We can also learn to speak life into others who need encouragement. As Scripture says, "the tongue has the power of life and death" (Prov 18:21). We must choose how we use our words.

I have always been intrigued by a man in the New Testament who was known for encouraging others. His given name was Joseph, but the Apostles nicknamed him "Barnabas," which means "son of encouragement." In Scripture, we see Barnabas (1) encouraging the poor (Acts 4) using his own money, (2) encouraging the marginalized (Acts 9) by helping an outsider feel like an insider, and (3) encouraging a quitter who needed a second chance (Acts 15). Barnabas inspires me to encourage people who are in these same situations today.

People everywhere get discouraged in their struggles with finances. Are we looking for opportunities to give encouragement? Perhaps we have cash to give—or time. Think how encouraged a single mom or a struggling young couple who have children would be by an offer of free babysitting. People around us are discouraged due to feeling marginalized because they lack resources; we just have to see them. In every group of people, some are at the margins, wondering whether they will ever be accepted. We must ask God to help us see them. Similarly, some people need a second chance—or perhaps a third, fourth, or fifth. Indeed, it is easy to get down on yourself when you blow it. At such times, we all need an encouraging word spoken by someone who believes in us. In my role as a professor, I have gotten to know several students who need both a word of encouragement and a second chance. I have students who have dealt with drug addiction, self-harm, sexual promiscuity, abortion, prison, and suicidal thoughts. And these are young people attending a *Christian* university. Think how many more have the same need outside the Church!

I was discouraged during my first year teaching at the college level, afflicted by a full-blown case of what some call "imposter syndrome." I often felt as if someone were stalking me, waiting to arrest me for impersonating a professor. Among the members of the faculty, I admired Dr. John Castelein in particular because of his academic training, his brilliant insights, and his teaching skills. He even had a Ph.D. in philosophy from the University of Chicago! One day he came up to me after a faculty meeting and said, "Mike, whenever you speak up in a faculty meeting, I always listen closely to what you have to say." He might not remember saying those words to me, but I have never forgotten them. They encouraged me at a time when I seriously doubted that I had what it took to be a real professor.

Encouraging words can also speak life in written form. I keep a file in my office labeled "Encouraging Mike." It is a file in which I put encouraging notes I have received over the years, all collected in one place to lift my spirit when I need it. This file comes in handy especially after I have given a poor lecture or when I wonder whether my teaching is making any difference. These notes are life-giving on days when I ask myself whether I should be in another line of work. And a few years ago, I decided to write people what I call "Barney notes." Like Barnabas in Scripture, I try to look around for someone who could use some encouragement, then write that person a short, encouraging note. The results have been profound. I have discovered that people love to get encouragement notes just as much as I do. We live in a society that constantly tears people down. Cutting sarcasm is our favorite style of humor. Paul charges Christians to not be conformed to the pattern of this world (Rom 12:2). He also challenged the Christians at Ephesus to "not let any unwholesome talk come out of your mouths, but only what is helpful for building others up" (Eph 4:29). If that Scripture were a regulation for television shows, sitcoms would disappear! In his letter to the Philippian church, Paul encourages the Christians to "do everything without complaining or arguing," making their lives "shine like stars in the universe" (Phil 2:14–15). We live in a society filled with complaining and arguing. If we Christians could stop complaining and arguing and instead become encouragers, we would stick out in a good way. Indeed, the contrast would be like that of diamonds on black velvet or shining stars on a clear night.

When I was a youth minister, I learned the power of encouragement from an idea I got out of a book of youth ministry ideas. It was called the "car wash." To hold a car wash, line students up in two parallel lines facing each other, then choose someone to walk through the car wash. As he or she passes through the car wash, each person on either side must give the "car" a compliment—no sarcasm or empty flattery allowed. Holding a car wash can be embarrassing at first, but it can be life-changing for a young person when done well.

I am consciously trying to become a more immediate application encourager. When I have a good thought about my wife, I now try to tell her right away rather than letting the moment pass and running the risk of forgetting to tell her later. I am trying to encourage people immediately—as soon as the Holy Spirit prompts me to do so, without allowing myself time to forget. Such promptings sometimes come in the middle of the night, when I wake up with someone on my mind. When I do, I pray for that person immediately, then—not wanting to text him or her at 3 a.m.—write that person's name on a notepad by my bed to remind me to text or email him or her in the morning.

As I write this chapter, I am in the final stages of writing the dissertation for my Ph.D. When I was just beginning doctoral classes, I ran into a former professor of mine, Dr. Rondal Smith, who has a Ph.D. in linguistics and who has traveled around the world as a consultant for Bible translation projects. He had been a great encouragement to me during my missionary career in the DR Congo. When I confessed to Dr. Smith my personal doubts about being able to finish the doctoral program, he replied, "Mike, if you can live in the DR Congo, then you can get a Ph.D.!" His words spoke life into me. I went home that night and wrote them on a yellow sticky note that I affixed to the bulletin board above my office desk. Mark Twain said, "I can live for two months on a good compliment"—and indeed, I believe that some compliments are powerful enough to keep us going for a lifetime!

Some compliments affect us so deeply that we don't need to write them on sticky notes to remember them; they are permanently written on our heart. One of the best compliments I ever received came from Max Lucado. I normally don't get to spend time with "famous Christians" such as Max, but I was asked to give a short invitation challenge, in front of thousands of people, immediately after Max spoke at a missionary convention. Max spoke for thirty minutes; I spoke for five. (Later, one of my students joked, "Hey, did you see Max Lucado up there on stage tonight, opening for Mike Nichols?") It was an amazing night. Dozens answered the call to become long-term missionaries. After the service, I held onto a folding chair in a secluded place behind the stage so that Max could stand on it to pray over the large group of people who had responded to the invitation.

But before that, after giving my five-minute challenge that night up on stage, I walked away from the podium, glancing back at Max. He gave me the thumbs-up sign and spoke two life-giving words to me: "Good job!" Even if he was just being polite, I will never forget those two little words of his. Later that evening, I also received some very unexpected encouraging words from my dad, who was also attending the convention. In the middle of a conversation, he said, "Mike, I don't think this will be the last time you speak in front of a large crowd of people." He said it almost as an aside, but I will remember his words forever. I received them deep in my soul—life-giving, powerful words of blessing from my father.

Life is too short not to take every opportunity to speak life into others.

LIFE APPLICATION

1. Who do you know right now who could use some encouragement? Someone contemplating dropping out of school? Leaving his or her marriage? Running away? Giving in to sexual pressures? Taking his or her own life? Being marginalized or bullied? Dealing with financial pressures? Send that person a special note of encouragement.

2. Reflect on 1 Corinthians 1:3–5. Where in your life have you received deep encouragement and comfort? Find a way to turn that into ministry to others. Begin keeping a file of encouraging notes that people have given you that you can review when you are feeling down.

3. Pray daily: "Lord, allow me to be a source of encouragement to the people whom you allow me to meet today."

CHAPTER 31

THE MENTORING LIFE

Life is too short not to pour yourself into others

"The things you have heard me say in the presence of many witnesses entrust to reliable men who will also be qualified to teach others."
2 Timothy 2:2

"Significance happens when we enable those around us to discover their own significance."
Earl Palmer

Everyone has special gifts, talents, abilities, and experiences. It would be a shame for you and I to go through life and not take the time to pour into others what we have received. I love the principle of equipping found in 2 Timothy 2:2. The Apostle Paul told his young protégé, Timothy, "The things you have heard me say in the presence of many witnesses entrust to reliable men who will also be qualified to teach others." The equipping principle of this verse creates an exponential multiplying effect, but only if those who are mentored are equipped to themselves be equippers of others. When this idea of continual, ongoing equipping is at its foundation, mentoring goes on for generations, affecting uncounted numbers of people.

Mentoring is also a way for the influence of your life to continue after you die. The month after Steve Szoke was diagnosed with cancer, he emailed his family and friends to talk about the power of mentoring:

I look at my daughter Jada and see so much potential for the Kingdom of God. One of my favorite things I've had the pleasure of doing in ministry is to develop and mentor students to step forward into ministry themselves. I am reminded of Roland, Jake, Tania, Mike and so many other students that are serving in a great capacity without the "minister" title. Jada; I believe and pray that Jada will not only follow in these students footsteps, not only follow in my footsteps, but be an even greater, bolder, more creative and more loving minister than myself.

Steve was constantly pouring himself into his daughter and into many students in his youth ministry. Roland, Jake, and Mike have all gone on to become "professional ministers" in three different churches. Jake and his wife, Tania, ended up ministering with the same church that Steve helped start, the Impact Christian Church in Merryville, Indiana. You could say that Jake stepped into the footsteps of his mentor Steve. The influence of Steve Szoke is continuing on in powerful ways through the lives of those he mentored.

I love what Steve said about how people can serve in great capacities without having the title "minister." Once, while preaching a revival at a small church, I decided to pass out a reminder of my sermon's main point, the priesthood of all believers, taken from 1 Peter 2:9: "But you are a chosen people, a royal priesthood, a holy nation, a people belonging to God, that you may declare the praises of him who called you out of darkness into his wonderful light." Our culture promotes an unbiblical separation of "sacred and secular," and nowhere more than in the church, where we ordain professional ministers or clergy, considering everyone else laity. I made some homemade clerical collars from white poster board and then, the end of my sermon, took off my tie and put one of the white strips of poster board in the collar of my blue shirt. I asked the congregation what I looked like; they responded, "A priest." Then I told them that I had a clerical collar to give to everyone at the door when we shook hands on their way out.

I dared them to wear the collars the following week—at their workplace, on their tractor, at the coffee shop, or while working around the house—to remind them that each of us is a priest. The Bible teaches that every follower of Christ is a minister—not just those who get paid to do ministry. Churches are full of members who don't realize that their "secular" jobs are places of ministry. Bob Lowery, one of my professors, used to say, "Your ordination to ministry is your baptism."

I love how Steve Szoke spoke about equipping his daughter for ministry. I have poured myself into my three children and am excited when I think of the ministry they are doing in their spheres of influence. My daughter Sarah is a licensed professional counselor. My son Jason works for a department of the U.S. Government as well as being a business manager for a medical clinic. My daughter Sammy mentors at-risk kids through a ranch/equestrian ministry. They are all priests of God; sometimes I am amazed to think of all the people they are influencing for the kingdom of God. But as excited as I am about what my kids are doing, I get even more pumped up when I think about my grandkids also being priests of God.

I love mentoring students at Lincoln Christian University. Every year, I volunteer to lead a small group of young men called a "spiritual formation group." I also lead a one-week off-campus missions/service trip each spring semester, which has allowed me to take groups of students to Poland, Mexico, Quebec, St. Louis, and Chicago. But sometimes mentoring can be as simple as taking one or more of my students with me on a teaching or speaking engagement. Sacred conversations often happen on the way or on the return trip in the car. I love teaching in the classroom, but I enjoy one-on-one mentoring outside the classroom as well. I am inspired every morning when I walk into my office and look at the world map on my wall: It is covered with the pictures of over seventy former students who are serving God on six continents in more than twenty-five countries. When you pour yourself into others, the influence of your life multiplies.

Mentoring should go both ways in your life. You need to pour into others, but you also need to be poured into. No matter your age, you should look for someone farther along the road in life (in age and spiritual maturity) who can give you advice and wisdom. I recently started meeting with three older men from my church who are all in their seventies; I am just starting my sixties. I call this monthly meeting my "sage breakfast." I meet with them in order to soak up wisdom for living. You can also be mentored by people who have gone before us when you read what they have written. I am working to read every book written by E. Stanley Jones and by Henri Nouwen, both deceased, but who remain powerful mentors in my life.

If you have a special skill of some kind, look for someone who wants to be trained in its use. Teaching is as simple as four easy steps: (1) You do it while they watch, (2) you do it while they help, (3) they do it while you help, and (4) they do it while you watch. You can teach anything from tying a shoe to public speaking using this approach.

One of the Church's weakest areas today is also one of its main purposes—making disciples who are themselves disciple-makers. Making converts or church members is easy, but making disciples who are disciple-makers is another thing entirely. We sometimes do well at the first part of the great commission—baptizing—but we need to improve on the second part: "teaching them to obey everything I have commanded them." Baptism, being a new birth, is only the beginning, not the end.

Churches have two major problems when it comes to new Christians. First is spiritual infanticide. We often leave new believers on their own after their baptism, expecting them to figure out the Christian life on their own somehow. We fail to mentor them and disciple them, neglecting to teach them how to obey the teachings of Christ. Doing so is like taking a newborn baby home from the hospital, lying it down on the couch, and saying, "The fridge is in the kitchen; help yourself if you get hungry. And the bathroom is down the hallway, on the right."

Moreover, many churches have become spiritual nurseries, full of immature, baby Christians who have never grown up. Members of some churches have been Christians for decades but have never matured. They were grumpy complainers when they were baptized, and thirty years later, they still are—they have not grown in joy. Some who were greedy when they got baptized have not grown in generosity fifty years later.

What is shocking is that no one seems to be surprised when believers don't grow up. When my granddaughter Gwen was 5 years old, I remember her running all over the house telling imaginative stories to her Grandpa Mike. I also remember holding her on the day she was born, when she weighed six pounds, thirteen ounces. At 5 years old, she weighed about fifty pounds and was about four feet tall—no baby any longer. But what would her parents have done had she failed to grow taller and heavier? What if she had not learned to crawl—or walk—or talk? They would have known something to be wrong. *Growth is evidence of life!* It is true with babies, and it is true with Christians.

To counter these problems, I made a simple vow when I was ministering at a small church in rural central Illinois: I would find a spiritual mentor for anyone I baptized. I would find a mature believer who was willing to mentor the new believer at least through his or her first year of being a Christian. The mentor would be someone who could teach the baby Christian how to pray, how to read the Bible, how to share his or her faith, and how to begin making needed character changes. Similarly, when I do premarital counseling, I have couples sign a covenant with me that requires them to find a mentoring married couple to help them during their first year of marriage. The mentoring couple will have been married for several years and can help the new couple through some of the bumps and adjustments that come during the first year of marriage. Even when I started my missionary career in the DR Congo, mentoring and equipping was my first priority. I didn't want to start anything that wouldn't be able to continue after I left. The Lord led me to pour myself into two Congolese young men who then became youth ministry trainers themselves. I am gratified to know that the youth ministries I helped to start in the DR Congo are now continuing without me—because of mentoring.

The influence of your life can last far beyond your death when you mentor others.

LIFE APPLICATION

1. What do you know how to do that you could train someone else to do? Create some kind of memory trigger to remind you to ask yourself before you fulfill a responsibility; who could accompany you or assist you in this responsibility?

2. Ask God to give you someone to mentor—someone into whom you can pour all that you are and know.

3. Ask God to give you a mentor—someone farther along the spiritual path than you are who could pour himself or herself into you.

CHAPTER 32

THE ACCOUNTABLE LIFE

Life is too short not to be held accountable for it

"As iron sharpens iron, so one man sharpens another."
Proverbs 27:17

*"Two are better than one, because they have a good return for
their work: If one falls down, his friend can help him up. But
pity the man who falls and has no one to help him up!"*
Ecclesiastes 4:9–10

We are not meant to "do" life by ourselves. Life is too short not to have deep friendships that can keep us accountable and on the right track. My first experience with an accountability partner was on the mission field. A missionary friend whom I'll call "Paul" was having some problems in his marriage. Paul had developed an emotional attachment with another female missionary but, praise God, had been confronted about the inappropriate relationship before it became sexualized. The leadership of his mission agency asked me to meet with him regularly to hold him accountable for his marriage. I began to meet weekly with Paul to ask him about how things were going in his marriage—whether the healthy boundaries that had been set up were being kept.

Things went well for a while, but then the Lord confronted me about the one-way accountability of our relationship. I had not been tempted to have an affair as Paul had been, but the Lord made it very clear that I needed healthy accountability in my own marriage just as much as Paul needed it for his marriage. I shared this conviction with Paul, and our relationship quickly evolved into a relationship of mutual accountability. I had never experienced this level of commitment in a relationship with another man. Having someone look me in the eye regularly to ask me how I was *really* doing was empowering and life-giving. I had never regularly confessed my weaknesses, sins, or vulnerabilities to anyone—including my wife. The experience was so helpful that when I left the mission field in 1993, I vowed to never allow myself to live for a long period outside a relationship of face-to-face accountability with another Christian brother. If the relationship must end when a person moved or when other circumstances of life interfered, then I would seek out another accountability relationship as soon as possible. I made this vow in 1993, and I have kept it for over twenty-five years. I will keep it until I die.

When I started teaching at Lincoln Christian University in 1994, I approached Marvin, the preacher at our church in Mt. Pulaski, Illinois, and asked him whether he would consider entering into that kind of regular accountability partnership. He readily agreed and told me that my offer to him was like giving water to a thirsty man. When Marvin left to go to another church, I was able to develop accountability relationships with the ministers that followed. When we would meet, we asked each other about all the roles we played and the relationships we had in life. We especially checked in with each other about our marriages and how we were doing with our eyes and thoughts and heart in regard to sexual temptation. Russell Willingham, in his book *Breaking Free*, says, "Growth and healing always have and always will come through relationships with God, self, and others." Because some of our biggest problems in life come from relational wounds, they have relational solutions.

I have found protective power by confiding in others and asking them to hold me accountable. This protective power can come from a one-on-one relationship or from a small group of men (I use both). For example, several years ago, before I traveled to a city on the east coast to teach an intensive class, knowing that I would be staying a couple nights in a hotel alone without my wife, I sought help from a group of men. I asked the small group of male students with whom I meet every week for spiritual formation to hold me accountable to abide by a rule I had made for myself when traveling alone. If I stay overnight in a hotel, I don't turn the television on at all—even to watch the news. I know I can't trust myself with a remote in my hand and cable television available. Sometimes I even put a towel over the television or place a picture of my family atop it to remind me of the boundary I have set. Knowing that six male students whom I was mentoring would ask me whether I turned on the television helped me keep up this hedge of protection.

A few years ago, I went on a forty-day trip to Africa to collect data for my doctoral dissertation. My wife was unable to accompany me. Worse, I had layovers in a European city both ways. Before leaving, I asked four men who are very close friends of mine—their names are Mark, Rob, David, and Tim—to hold me accountable for what I would do and see during my trip. Knowing that I would be reporting to these four dear brothers helped empower my resolve to protect myself from any potential sexual temptation.

Proverbs 17:10 says, "A rebuke impresses a man of discernment." Wise people give other people permission to rebuke them. Living the accountable life means listening to and receiving live-giving rebuke. Accountability partnerships are not two people policing each other trying to catch the other in the act so that they can be punished. Accountability partnerships are relationships of permission and blessing. You are giving another person permission to ask you hard questions, to call you out on things, and to get in your face if needed. The motive behind this is deep love. Truly loving someone requires both tender and tough love. A true friend doesn't let his friend ruin his life and slide into hell. I love what John Eldredge says in his book *Wild at Heart*, "we need fellow warriors, someone to fight alongside, someone to watch our back."

Our culture is one of our problems. We are so individualistic that we consider religion to be a private affair. When God asked Cain where his brother was, Cain mockingly responded, "Am I my brother's keeper?" Anyone who reads the Bible seriously will know that God answers such questions, from Genesis to Revelation, with an unequivocal "Yes!" I officiated a wedding for two of my students during which I challenged the bridesmaids and groomsmen to shoulder their responsibility for the couple. I told them that standing up at a wedding is not merely a time to get all dressed up for wedding pictures; it is a way of saying, "I will promise to be an advocate for this marriage, and I will hold the couple accountable for the vows they are making on their wedding day." The Christian life is to be lived in authentic community, including through accountability. We really do need each other—saying so isn't just words.

I have recently entered into a deeper level of accountability with a good friend. He texts me twice a week to tell me how he is doing with his marriage, describing sexual temptation as it comes in various forms. He has been brutally honest with me, sharing with me the times he leaves himself open to temptation—even when he doesn't fall into sin. He is becoming good at recognizing his old patterns and rationalizations and confesses when he knows that he is "thinking about" doing something wrong. For example, the other night he sent me this text:

Last night at the hotel I checked to see what was on HBO. Fortunately nothing tempting was on and I didn't check again. I wouldn't have watched anything for long because of the possibility of my wife waking and seeing. My past M.O. would be to scroll through the channel to catch "innocent" glimpses. But it was an old pattern and my guard was down because of the long, exhausting fight I had with my wife that day. I am thankful I caught no glimpses, but I wanted to drag it into the light with you. It bothers me that I left myself open like that.

I love this brother deeply, and I will try to follow his example when I send him accountability texts. One of the best questions that a partner can ask is "If Satan were going to disqualify you from service in God's Kingdom right now, knowing your weaknesses, how would he do it?"

Something is very powerful about being in an accountability relationship that involves full disclosure. On the one hand, being fully known by another person can seem very risky; on the other, such a relationship can be one of the most empowering in life. Deep friendships such as these are some of life's greatest treasures: Life is too short not to discover the treasure of the accountable life.

LIFE APPLICATION

1. Do you have anyone in your life who holds you accountable? Would you be willing to make a life vow to never live without an accountability partner?

2. Who might be a potential accountability partner for you? What character qualities are you looking for in an accountability partner?

3. Think of some accountability questions that could be especially helpful to you if someone were to ask you them regularly. Ask God for the courage to be open about your weak areas, including old patterns of behavior that have led you into sin.

CHAPTER 33

THE WITNESSING LIFE

Life is too short to keep Jesus to yourself

*"You will be my witnesses in Jerusalem, and in all
Judea and Samaria, and to the ends of the earth."*
Acts 1:8

"Live your life in such a way it demands an explanation."
Unknown

Because Jesus is the savior of the world, life on Earth is too short to keep him to yourself. When I first began teaching at the college level, I taught a course on evangelism. One day, as I was walking out of class, I noticed one of my students sobbing her eyes out. I stopped to see what was wrong. Through bitter tears of regret, she told me that a high school friend of hers had been killed in a car accident. Over and over she said, "I never talked to her about Jesus!" I was reminded of how I felt when, as a student in college, I heard that a high school friend of mine had been killed in a car accident. I had been friendly with Brad, had played baseball and basketball with him and joked around with him—but I couldn't ever remember having directly talked to him about Jesus.

I once attended a funeral visitation for a young man who had died in a motorcycle accident. His life had mostly been about partying; everyone was well aware that he had no relationship with Jesus. Attending that visitation was one of the saddest things I have ever done. Behind the facade of photographs and memories of this young man stood a harsh and hopeless reality: He died with no hope beyond the grave. I left mourning for him and the members of his family, some of whom were dedicated Christians. I also left with feelings of regret, wondering whether I could have done a better job witnessing to him. I had talked to him only on a couple occasions, and I don't remember having ever mentioned Jesus to him. Life is too short to live with regrets about our testimony for Jesus Christ.

Every Christian is called to be a witness for Jesus Christ. Doing so is not optional, not only for those who have "the gift of evangelism." Testifying about Jesus Christ is difficult in a society that values pluralism. Christians make absolute claims about life and death and salvation—claims that come directly from the mouth of Jesus. No one can misunderstand his clear statement "I am the way and the truth and the life. No one comes to the Father except through me" (John 14:6). The Apostle Peter told the Jewish leaders in Jerusalem that "salvation is found in no one else, for there is no other name under heaven given to men by which we must be saved" (Acts 4:12). So how can we go about being a witness for Jesus in a society that denies claims of exclusive truth from the get-go?

I have been helped by the advice of E. Stanley Jones, a missionary to India who lived during the twentieth century. I read about something profound that happened to him when he preached his very first sermon at his hometown church. He had studied and studied in his sermon preparation, wanting to "argue well for God" when he preached. He memorized his sermon word for word. But, being nervous, he started out talking with his voice at a rather high pitch, then made a slip of the tongue, using a nonsensical word. At that, a young girl in the congregation visibly lowered her head, struggling not to laugh aloud.

When Jones saw her reaction, his mind went blank—he forgot everything he was going to say. After an awkward silence, he began walking back to his seat, only for the Lord to speak to his heart, asking, "Haven't I done anything for you?" Jones responded, "Yes, of course—you have given me life itself." Then the Lord prompted him: "Well, why don't you just say that?" Jones didn't go back to his seat; instead, he described what God had done in his life. Several of those attending that day were moved by his story, one of whom even dedicated himself to overseas missionary service.

E. Stanley Jones saw that event as a paradigm change in his conception of what it meant to be a Christian minister. He decided that he did not want to try to be God's lawyer, arguing for God. No, he reasoned, God is big enough to argue for himself. Rather, Jones began to see himself as a witness, one testifying about the working of God's grace in an unworthy life.

Every believer has a unique testimony, a unique story of his or her experience with God. I used to think that my testimony was nothing special—that it was kind of boring, actually. I wasn't saved from a life of crime or addiction to drugs or any such thing; certainly my testimony wasn't a very dramatic one. But later I realized that *every* believer's testimony is dramatic and powerful: It is the story of God's grace saving a lost sinner, one who was spiritually dead. I now see my testimony as my most powerful tool for evangelism.

Testimonies are effective for many reasons. First, every testimony is unique, like a person's fingerprints or DNA. Someone might call his or her testimony boring, but that just isn't true. Every person has had a unique experience with the living God. Moreover, testimonies are true stories—they really happened. Think of the difference between going to a movie that came straight from a screenwriter's imagination and a film based on a true story— the latter affects us more deeply. Moreover, because our stories are real, they are not easily discredited. I don't have to memorize lots of Scripture or use a theological chart when I witness; I simply tell my story. It is a story I always have with me, and I can give it in any form—a two-minute version or a two-hour version, whatever the circumstance calls for.

Be careful if you are tempted to leave something out of your story. You never know what element of your story might connect with someone else. Especially don't leave out the "bad stuff." When we talk openly about our sin, as well as the times when we have been sinned against, people are drawn to us. There is something powerful about the transparency and vulnerability we exhibit when we share our stories. That's because every Christian is a broken person who is in the process of being healed by Jesus. The abuse I suffered as a boy is part of my story—I was emotionally abused by my father and sexually abused by an older family friend. Part of me very much wants to edit those parts out of my story, hiding them from others. But when I find the courage to share my own struggles, my transparency draws other people not only to me, but also to Christ. I love the "full circle" dynamic shown in 2 Corinthians 1:3–4:

Praise be to the God and Father of our Lord Jesus Christ, the Father of compassion and the God of all comfort, who comforts us in all our troubles, *so that we can comfort those in any trouble with the comfort we ourselves have received from God.*

Of course, the best-case scenario for witnessing is when someone asks you to explain yourself. I call it the million-dollar question: *Why?* When we live in such a way that our words and deeds get someone's attention, our behavior creates the ultimate context for powerful witness. When someone asks, "Why were you so nice to me?" or "Why don't you swear and tell dirty stories like everyone else?" a door is open for our testimony. We can open the door even farther by responding, "Do you *really* want to know why?" When they say that they do, then we tell them our story—and Jesus's. Accept the challenge to *live your life in such a way that it demands an explanation.*

The word *evangelism* has gotten a bad rap among both believers and nonbelievers. Many associate the word with high-pressure salesmanship, cramming Jesus down someone's throat. But the word actually means to "announce good news." I ask myself, *Why I am tempted to keep the best news in the world to myself?* Good news is meant to be shared. A witness simply relates what he or she has seen or experienced. You are a witness to what the Lord has done in your life, and no one can testify about that better than you can! Some people among your circle of influence are more open to *your witness* than they would be to testimony given by Billy Graham, Rick Warren, or Mother Teresa. Why? Because your friends don't know them; *they know you.*

God is building a family who will live with him forever, and he wants to include as many people in it as possible, from every language and ethnic group in the world. How amazing to think that God is giving us a part in his grand story of the ages! Paul says that you and I are "God's ambassadors": God is making his appeal to the world through us. Think about Jesus's words in Acts 1:8, when he says that we will be his witnesses in Jerusalem, Judea, and Samaria—and to the ends of the Earth. Jesus himself went to Jerusalem, Judea, and Samaria—but then he handed the torch to his disciples. And we are among them: We get to continue the mission of Jesus on Earth. Life is too short to keep Jesus to ourselves!

LIFE APPLICATION

1. Think about all the people in your circle of influence who don't know Jesus. What keeps you from witnessing to them? If you are having a hard time coming up with names, ask God to show you people in your life to whom he wants you to testify about Jesus.

2. Make a "high five list"—a list of five nonbelievers for whose salvation you will pray daily. Put the list where you will see it every day. Pray in particular that God will bring believers into their lives who will boldly testify about Jesus's power.

3. When was the last time you shed tears over someone who doesn't know Jesus? Ask God to break your heart for the lost. Ask him to give

you his eyes with which to see the world. Every day, ask God to give you opportunities to be a witness for him.

CHAPTER 34

THE CALLED LIFE

Life is too short to miss your calling

"The man who enters by the gate is the shepherd of his sheep ... he goes on ahead of them, and his sheep follow him because they know his voice."
John 10:2-4

"Are you a called person or a driven person?"
Gordon McDonald

How regrettable to reach the end of your life still wondering about its purpose! Many people seem to get stuck earning a paycheck, eating, sleeping, spending the paycheck, and then starting the cycle all over again. But life is more than earning money and spending it. Inside every person, something asks, *Why am I here? What is my purpose? What is my calling?* At the end of their lives, most people don't say, "I'm really glad I played it safe, taking no chances." Instead, I have heard people talk about having regrets, wishing they had taken more risks—wishing they had chased their dreams.

I almost missed my calling by having screwed-up theology. One day, sitting in a college class, I thought to myself how cool it would be to be a professor in a Christian university someday. But when I had that thought, I suffered immediate emotional backlash. In what seemed like an instant, my emotions transitioned from excited joy to a cold critique of my motives. An inner voice spoke to me clearly and firmly, saying, *Well, if that is something you want, then it certainly couldn't be God's will for you!*

I have to recognize that statement as nothing more than a satanic lie. In speaking about the sheep (people) of his fold, Jesus said, "the thief comes only to steal and kill and destroy" (John 10:10). As I look back on over twenty-five years of being a professor at a Christian university, I shiver to think of all the good things that Satan wanted to steal from me. God has used my calling as a professor to shape and mentor a new generation of missionaries who are serving all over the world. No wonder Satan wanted me to view my desire to be a professor as nothing more than selfishness.

I think of the whole area of calling as frontline spiritual warfare. The Apostle Peter says, "You are a chosen people, a royal priesthood, a holy nation, a people belonging to God, that you may declare the praises of him who called you out of darkness into his wonderful light" (1 Pet 2:9). Satan will do everything he can to stop us from messing with people in his kingdom of darkness—he doesn't want to give up anyone from his kingdom. Every Christian's calling from God is connected to this very real spiritual battle for the souls of men. One of Satan's biggest lies is that evangelism is for only those who are professionally "called" to the ministry as preachers or missionaries, having nothing to do with those called to business, education, medicine, or raising kids.

As I have mentioned, my theology began being corrected when I started having children. When I reflect on what goes on in my heart when one of my kids opens a birthday gift, I see clearly something in my heart that wants to give my child his or her heart's desire. As I connected the source of my feelings as a daddy to the heart of my heavenly Father, I began to believe the truth of Matthew 7:11. Our heavenly Father is the one who desires to "give good gifts to those who ask him." David exhorts, "Praise the LORD, O my soul … who satisfies your desires with good things" (Ps 103:1, 5). Certainly we can have selfish motives (see James 4:3), and undoubtedly God is not going to give us something that will ultimately hurt or spoil us, but this basic desire—of a father wanting to give his child that child's greatest desire—comes directly from the father heart of God!

One memorable Christmas, when my daughter Sammy was a young girl, the generosity of a friend allowed my wife and me to give her the present that was her heart's desire—a horse. I put Sammy in the back seat of the car and blindfolded her, then drove her through the country to one of our neighbors' barns. I will never forget the look on Sammy's face when we took the blindfold off to reveal her new horse. She was speechless for a couple minutes, something that had never happened before. But her face was saying, *I can't believe it. This is exactly what I wanted!*

My theological perspective on God's will and calling for me has changed from thinking that something that I desire could not be something that God desires for me, to realizing that many times, the two are actually the same thing. As I look back on a quarter century of teaching at a Christian university, I feel God smiling at me, and I think of the scene in *Chariots of Fire* in which Olympic runner Eric Liddell tries to explain his passion about running to his sister: "When I run, I feel God's pleasure!" When I teach and mentor undergraduate students, I feel God's pleasure. And when I think that I almost missed my calling through faulty theology, I shiver.

Reflecting on life's brevity, including by thinking about our impending death, can motivate us to find our calling. In particular, I have found the following seven questions helpful when it comes to discerning the calling of God:

1. *Am I living out my primary calling to God himself?*

   Calling can be a very mysterious concept for some. In a general way, the Bible describes the life purpose of every Christian. We need to start with the *great commandment* in Matthew 22 (to love God first). This is a commandment for every Christian—everyone is called to love God.

2. *Do I see the bigger picture of what God is doing?*

   We also need to look at another Scripture that is meant for every Christian, the *great commission* given in Matthew 28—to make disciples of all nations. Throughout Scripture, we see God's desire to bless all nations. Every disciple in every age lives under the command to make more disciples, no matter that disciple's vocation.

3. *Am I seeking the guidance of the Holy Spirit?*

   The Holy Spirit comes alongside the disciple as a "counselor" (John 14:16), giving guidance. Jesus assured his disciples that the Spirit would "teach you all things" (John 14:26), calling the Spirit the "Spirit of truth" who will "guide you into all truth" (John 16:13).

4. *Have I received confirmation from others?*

   God can even use people whom we don't know to confirm his call in our life. Think of how God used Ananias to explain and confirm God's call for the Apostle Paul. Of course, God can also use individuals with whom we already have a relationship, such as Paul for Timothy, to confirm our direction.

5. *Have I looked within myself for clues to my calling?*

   By God's design, we are individuals, each of us having unique life experiences, personal abilities, and spiritual gifts. We should be encouraged to realize that God can use even our bad life experiences for his glory. Paul told the Corinthian church that the reason why we are comforted by God in all our troubles is so that we can comfort others (2 Cor 1:3–5). Which of your life experiences might be preparing you for ministry?

6. *Do I know an "open door" when I see one?*

    We cannot put limitations on God's way of calling people, but we can discern certain themes from Scripture. Often the need is part of the call. Many Christians pray for God to "open doors" for them to proclaim the gospel, meaning "make it easy for me to proclaim the gospel" or "take away all the obstacles standing in the way of my proclaiming the gospel." But Paul writes about open doors in the context of opposition. In 1 Corinthians 16:8–9, he says, "But I will stay on at Ephesus until Pentecost, because a great door for effective work has opened to me, and *there are many who oppose me.*" In Colossians 4:3, Paul says, "Pray for us, too, that God may open a door for our message, so that we may proclaim the mystery of Christ, *for which I am in chains.*" Professor Chris DeWelt provides insight into these passages, saying, "The open door Paul is talking about is probably an open door *for them*, not for us!" Don't equate God's missionary calling with a lack of obstacles.

7. *Am I being honest with myself?*

    We need to become honest about our motives, fears, and excuses when it comes to discerning our calling. Are we motivated by a desire for adventure, driven by guilt, or eager to see God worshiped among the nations? Author Thomas Hale lists six motivations that often constitute false calls: (1) the desire to meet other people's expectations, (2) the desire to prove your worth, (3) the desire for a change of scene, (4) the desire to earn favor with God, (5) a feeling of guilt, and (6) aroused emotions alone.

If we develop an intimate relationship with God, the issue of "calling" will probably take care of itself! Jesus never promised to show us the way, to show us the next five years of our lives, or to give us a map to follow. He simply said *I am the way—follow me.*

LIFE APPLICATION

1. If you are sure of your calling, write it out in one or two sentences, then put it where you will see it daily.

2. Have you dismissed one of your big dreams by calling it selfishness? What makes you feel most alive? When do you feel God's pleasure most?

3. Which of the seven questions about calling is the most difficult for you to answer in the affirmative? How about the easiest? Does God want to use a painful experience from your life as a doorway to ministry?

CHAPTER 35

THE WARFARE LIFE
Life is too short not to battle Satan's lies

*"For our struggle is not against flesh and blood, but against the rulers,
against the authorities, against the powers of this dark world and
against the spiritual forces of evil in the heavenly realms."*
Ephesians 6:12

*"Be self-controlled and alert. Your enemy the devil prowls
around like a roaring lion looking for someone to devour."*
1 Peter 5:8

Every day of life on Earth is a day of spiritual warfare. Life is too short not to realize that we are daily in battle with a real enemy. Our enemy Satan has one main objective: our destruction. We would be foolish to enter each day unaware of Satan's schemes directed against us. Someday, Satan will be cast into the lake of fire, but until then, every day is a fight. The first thing we must do is understand our adversary. *Satan* means "adversary or enemy," and *devil* means "accuser or slanderer." I like to use the acronym MAL to describe Satan's basic character: He is a murderer, an accuser, and a liar. We know the prefix *mal* from many words, among them *malnutrition* and *malpractice*; it simply means *bad*. Satan is a bad character in every sense of the word—he is filled with evil. In John 8:44, Jesus says that Satan was a "murderer from the beginning" and calls him the "father of lies." The Apostle Paul says that Satan is such a good liar that he "masquerades as an angel of light" (2 Cor 11:14). In Revelation 12:10, Satan is also called the "accuser of our brethren" (KJV).

Anyone who can make himself sound like an angel, a very messenger of God, has got to be the biggest and best liar there has ever been. Jesus said that whenever Satan speaks, he speaks in his mother tongue—lies. A friend of mine said something about Satan a few years ago that I have never forgotten: "It always seems as if Satan gets away with at least one big lie with every person." I know well that Satan or one of his demons has whispered to me for years, lies that I have believed. Of the many serious battlegrounds for spiritual warfare in the world and in the unseen realm, one of the biggest is the space between our ears—the mind.

Our enemy also doesn't fight fair. He knows our weaknesses—our Achilles heel—and he attacks during our weakest moments. Use the acronym H.A.L.T.S. to remind yourself of some of Satan's favorite times to attack—when we are hungry, angry, lonely, tired, or sick. I heard a speaker say, "Satan knows it only takes one unguarded Saturday night to ruin your life." Satan's goal is to destroy you, and he continues to prowl around, looking for a chance to pounce on you and devour you (1 Pet 5:8). The Bible presents Satan as a formidable opponent, but we must not adopt an unbalanced theology concerning his power. His power is limited. He is stronger than you and I are on our own, but he isn't even close to being as strong as God is. He and God are in different categories. Satan is a created being, a fallen archangel—but God is creator. A fight between God and Satan wouldn't be a fight: The Bible tells us that when Satan's time is over, God sends him to the lake of fire with one simple command. God and Satan fighting would not resemble two men of similar strengths having a boxing match. It would be like a man fighting an ant: At any moment, the man could crush the ant using a single finger.

We must be careful not to underestimate or overestimate our enemy. We would be foolish to ignore Satan and his schemes against us, living as if he doesn't exist. But we would be equally foolish to view him as having too much power, causing us to live in constant fear of him. Similarly, C. S. Lewis in his book *Screwtape Letters*, warns us of two errors into which we can fall:

There are two equal and opposite errors into which our race can fall about the devils. One is to disbelieve in their existence. The other is to believe, and to feel an excessive and unhealthy interest in them. They themselves are equally pleased by both errors and hail a materialist or a magician with the same delight.

Perhaps you have fallen into Satan's subtle trap and do not believe that he exists—or perhaps you think that he exists, but you don't give his existence much thought. If so, then you are in real danger, for Satan is real, and you are underestimating a powerful enemy. But equally, if you live in paralyzing fear of Satan, then you have the opposite problem: You are overestimating his power.

We need to see how hideous and dark the ways of Satan are. We are not to hate people, but we are commanded to hate evil. Psalm 97:10 says, "Let those who love the LORD *hate evil*." Proverbs 8:13 says, "To fear the LORD is to *hate evil*." Romans 12:9 tells us, "Love must be sincere. *Hate what is evil*; cling to what is good." Satan is filled with evil, and although we are not commanded in Scripture to hate Satan himself, we are commanded to hate his evil ways. Recently I saw how hideous and evil Satan's lies have been to my wife. I hated it so much for how he had lied to my wife that I cursed at him on my drive to work because of the one big lie he had been telling her over and over again for more than forty years. Ever since Julie's dad left her mom for another woman when Julie was a young teenager, she has been living with an abandonment wound. Satan loves to use this wound to lie to her. He wants her to feel worthless, useless, and abandoned. For some reason, the enormity and longevity of the lie made me mad as hell that day. In a loud voice, I told God to damn Satan to hell, and I told Satan to get his evil claws out of my wife. It's a good thing I was traveling down a country road: No other drivers were there to see me having what probably looked like a bad case of road rage! From that day on, I have had a new resolve in my heart to fight for the healing of my wife's heart.

Satan was fighting for Steve Szoke's heart and soul in a major way during Steve's battle with cancer. Just six weeks before Steve lost his earthly battle with cancer, he wrote about Satan's whispers to him:

I also know, that just as Satan is whispering in my ear, he may be in yours as well. Satan has been gently lying saying, "God has abandoned Steve." My God is still right here with me. I made a statement the other day to a fellow minister. I said, "I cannot fathom the mind of God. I don't know what His plans are, I don't know why I have this disease. I cannot grasp His mind in this. I can, however, fathom and understand His heart. Just as much as I am broken about this, as my wife, as my parents are broken about this, God's heart breaks for this as well." My God is still my Father, my God is still my refuge and my God is still the one true Rock that I will ever cling to.

Praise God that Steve did not believe Satan's whispers to him. Steve never doubted the love of his heavenly father, not to the very end of his life on Earth.

I have heard many different whispers from Satan over my lifetime. One of his most persistent whispers has been, *Mike, you keep on sinning. God is tired of forgiving you—he can't use you in ministry any longer.* Another one I have heard often is, *Mike, you don't know what you are doing. Your incompetency invalidates your ability to do ministry for God.* I know now that both of these lies smell like smoke because they come from the pit of hell, but they are still hard to counter. The main reason why fighting these kind of lies is so difficult is that they are partially true. Satan is a master at taking truth and twisting it for his purposes. He is an expert at using half-truths. But I have learned an effective strategy for battling these "half-truth" lies. It is based on the principle of "agreeing with your adversary." When two people are in an argument and one person decides to agree with the other, the argument is over. The first step, then, is to agree with the part of Satan's accusation against you that is true. Then you must quickly remind Satan of the whole truth.

An example of a warfare conversation in the battlefield of my mind might go something like this:

Satan: "Mike, you sin too much to be used by God."

Mike: "You are absolutely right, Satan, when you say that I am a sinner and that I sin too much. But thanks for reminding me that I don't relate to God based on my sin. I am a sinner saved by God's grace, as the Bible says in Ephesians 2:8."

Or perhaps this:

Satan: "Mike, you are incompetent. You can't serve God."

Mike: "You are absolutely right, Satan, when you say that I am unable to do much using my own abilities. But thanks for reminding me that God is my competency, just as the Bible says in 2 Corinthians 3:5."

Notice that I used the truth of Scripture to battle Satan. I learned this from Jesus himself, in Matthew 4. When Satan tempted Jesus to turn stones into bread or to throw himself down from the temple, Jesus used Scripture to put Satan in his place. The word of God is called the "sword of the Spirit," and the Bible tells us to use it to battle Satan (Eph 6:17). The next verse tells us to "pray in the Spirit on all occasions with all kinds of prayers" (Eph 6:18). Prayer is one of our greatest weapons in fighting Satan, because it connects us with God. Satan is real, and he is powerful—more powerful than you or I—but he is in not more powerful than God, so we must stay connected to God in prayer and authentic relationship. Romans 8:31 says, "If God is for us, who can be against us?" Ephesians 6 lists seven pieces of spiritual armor that we must wear when battling Satan: the belt of truth, the breastplate of righteousness, the boots of the gospel of peace, the shield of faith, the helmet of salvation, the sword of the spirit (the word of God), and prayer. If we can wear this God-given armor daily, we will continue to stand in our battles with Satan. We would be foolish to rush into battle each day unarmed and without protection. We must get up every morning and dress for battle, for the normal Christian life is not a playground: it is a battleground.

Satan is a defeated enemy thanks to the death and resurrection of Jesus Christ, but during our time on Earth, Satan has been given limited freedom. If we submit ourselves to God and resist Satan, the Bible tells us that Satan will flee from us (Jas 4:7). We need to be alert about Satan's schemes against us so that we can resist him. The King James Version translates the first phrase of Ephesians 6:12 as "We wrestle not against flesh and blood." Wrestling is a good metaphor for spiritual battle, for wrestling has no timeouts. In the same way, we don't get to take a break from spiritual warfare: At no time is the battle not on. We will continue to wrestle with Satan until we die. Life is too short not to continually battle our real enemy.

LIFE APPLICATION

1. How can you remind yourself that you are in a daily spiritual battle against Satan and his demons? What are some of Satan's specific schemes or plans against you, against your family, against your ministry, and against your church?

2. Read the list of spiritual armor in Ephesians 6. Which piece of armor are you missing? Write out some specific warfare prayers that you can memorize and use at a moment's notice. Memorize specific passages of Scripture to use when Satan whispers lies to you.

3. Do you hate evil? Does any evil make you sick enough to make you want to do something about it? Do you need to ask God to help increase your hatred of evil?

CHAPTER 36

THE WORSHIPING LIFE

Life is too short to worship only on Sunday

"Therefore, I urge you, brothers, in view of God's mercy, to offer your bodies as living sacrifices, holy and pleasing to God—this is your spiritual act of worship."
Romans 12:1

"And whatever you do, whether in word or deed, do it all in the name of the Lord Jesus, giving thanks to God the Father through him."
Colossians 3:17

In true worship, we surrender our lives to God to serve him forever. Indeed, life is too short to call yourself a Christian without understanding the true meaning of worship. Worship is not something you do on Sunday morning for a couple hours—that activity would be better described as attending a corporate "worship service." We do not worship God only once a week, in a church building. We worship God every day of every week, all year long—no matter where we are. Many people treat worshiping God as they do being a member of a club, seeing the church as a clubhouse where they attend meetings, pay their dues, and hear the president announce the club's activities.

Worship is about God, not about us. In true worship, we put aside our preoccupations and focus on God. In the original languages of the Bible (Hebrew, Greek, and Aramaic), a dozen different words can be translated "worship" in English. The most frequently used means "bow down" or "fall prostrate." When we focus on God and get a glimpse of who he really is, bowing down and falling prostrate make sense. When I was a Christian college student, a visiting chapel speaker asked us what we would do if Jesus Christ—God in the flesh—came walking down the aisle toward the front. He asked whether we would go up and talk to him: Would we maybe shake his hand? Would we give him a high five? Then he demonstrated what he thought he would do—and immediately fell totally prostrate on the floor.

A missionary friend related an encounter he had with a little Ukrainian Jewish girl who was attending a church camp he was leading in Poland. During one lesson about the Ten Commandments, the teacher described how God talked with Moses: in a very loud voice, like thunder. When the teacher asked, "What would you do if God were to speak to you like that?" And the little girl was honest: "I think I would pee my pants!" She understood, perhaps for the first time, what being in the presence of an all-mighty God would be like. In true worship, we see God. When we gather corporately to worship God but don't see him in all his power, glory, and sovereignty, then perhaps we have only gathered with other people, sung some songs, shook a few hands, and listened to someone speak. We did a lot of things, but have we worshiped God?

In corporate worship, we are often betrayed by the structure of the building and the setup of the furniture, by chairs all facing the same way and by an elevated stage. The whole setup tempts us to think of worship as we do other corporate assemblies, such as in a gym for a basketball game or in an auditorium for a concert. In these settings, we divide people in two groups: players and spectators, or performers and audience. Sitting in a corporate worship service, we can easily think of ourselves as spectators and the worship team or the preacher as the performers. But in worship we are all performers before an audience of one—God. The important questions to ask about corporate worship are not whether it was "good" or whether it "did something" for us, but whether our own worship honored God. The key to worship is focusing on God.

The first of the Ten Commandments is clear: There is only one God, and we are to worship him alone. The meaning of the second commandment used to be a little fuzzy for me. I knew it prohibited the making of an idol, but I also thought I didn't have a problem with that one—I had never carved a wooden idol with my pocketknife and placed it atop the fireplace mantel. But after studying this commandment, I realized that I am constantly tempted to break this commandment—perhaps more than I am all the others combined! The first commandment prohibits the worship of false gods, but the second prohibits *the false worship of the true God*. In it, God says that we must take him exactly as he is, without ever trying to change him. When we try to change God, we are trying to whittle him down to size—to reduce, restrict, or shrink him. But God says, *Don't ever try to make an image of me, for such an image would be distorted and small. If you want to worship me, you must take me as I am.*

Our culture tells us that we can "have things our way," but God refuses to be shaped by us. As I reflect on the exalted, all-powerful, awesome, majestic—even terrifying—God described at Mt. Sinai, I begin to ask myself whether I have created a more comfortable image of God to worship: a smaller, safer, less demanding God—a more predictable God, one that I can control. I may not have carved an idol from wood or stone, but I have created an idol in my mind nonetheless—an image that is not the true God but only a caricature: a fiction. Imagine our audacity in thinking that we can reduce, restrict, or shape God to our standards. It has been said that God created man in his image—and then man returned the favor by creatng God in man's image.

The following are some "images of God" that we in America worship:

911 God: *God is for crises; I don't need him at other times.*
Grandpa God: *God passes out wise advice and treats—and he never spanks.*
Genie God: *God is the great wish-fulfiller in the sky, always ready to fulfill my every wish. He must act when I ask him to heal, deliver, and protect.*
"Let's Make a Deal" God: *God will do something for me if I promise to do something for him.*
Red, White, and Blue God: *God always acts in America's interest.*

We have been guilty of creating a God who is "there for me" instead of ourselves being there for God. Many of us are worshiping a God who is too small, a God of our own making. We have all been guilty of trying to trim the claws of the lion of the tribe of Judah. Instead, we must become like the children in C. S. Lewis's *Chronicles of Narnia,* who knew that Aslan was a good lion—but not a tame lion. We have become too familiar with the Holy Other, too casual with the creator of the universe. Because God is all-powerful, we must approach him with reverent fear and awe. But at the same time, we do not fear God as if he were an evil monster. God is good, and God is love—which is why he sacrificed Jesus on the cross to make a way for us to return to him.

We have another problem with our worship: the sacred–secular divide in our culture. We often think of things such as going to church, reading the Bible, and singing Christian songs as "sacred" activities but of things such as going to sporting events, reading the newspaper, and washing the dishes as "secular" activities. Colossians 3:17 says, "And *whatever you do,* whether in word or deed, do it all *in the name of the Lord Jesus,* giving thanks to God the Father through him." The phrase *whatever you do* covers a lot of things—in fact, every activity that we think of as either secular or sacred can go in that box.

And doing these things "in the name of Jesus" is another way of describing worship. What does it mean to do things "in the name of Jesus"? Sometimes we treat that phrase as a formula to be tagged onto the end of prayers. Biblically, however, doing something in Jesus's name can mean at least three things: First, acting *for his glory*, not our own or anyone else's. Second, doing things *by his strength* or authority, not our own. (For example, we read about people being healed from a disease or delivered from a demon "in Jesus name.") Third, doing things *the way that Jesus would do them*. Names in Bible times meant something, signifying a person's nature or character. Thus, doing something in Jesus's name means doing it the way he would. When we understand that we are supposed to do literally everything in Jesus's name, then anything from driving a car to cleaning a toilet becomes an act of worship—and worship then becomes as much what we do on Monday morning or Friday night as what we do on Sunday morning.

Another key to worship is the condition of our hearts—are we fully surrendered to God? In Psalm 51, David talks about the rituals of Old Testament worship, which included offering sacrifices. He realizes that animal sacrifice was not God's true desire: God wanted his heart. Indeed, a broken and contrite heart is what God looks for from us all. A friend of mine pointed out to me the difference between "making a commitment" to God and "totally surrendering" to God. When we talk about "making a commitment" to God, we often see it as "our commitment," something we can give—and take back. We make a commitment when we feel like doing so, knowing that we can always take it back when we want to. But total surrender is something different. Surrendering to God means giving your whole self to God for your whole life without limitation.

Not too many gestures are universal, but one that seems to be is the raising of one's hands in the air as a sign of surrender. When you raise your hands to God in true worship, you say *I surrender all—I offer you my whole life.* Some of the purest worship in which I have ever taken part was in fall

1979, at a missions conference in El Paso, Texas. During an invitation after one of the main sessions, I felt as if my heart were burning inside my chest. I went forward and raised my hands to God, saying with my whole heart, *Here am I Lord—send me!* I laid my life on the altar, saying *Lord, I will go anywhere you want me to go!* Worshiping means doing this every single day during the few days God gives us on Earth.

LIFE APPLICATION

1. What reminders can you put in your life to call you to surrender to God daily and worship him? How can you remove your focus from yourself and focus on God instead?

2. How are you tempted to change God, shaping him to make him easier for you to worship?

3. How can you remind yourself of the purpose of worship when you take part in a corporate worship service each Sunday? How can you remind yourself that you are still worshiping God even after you leave the church building?

CHAPTER 37

THE SABBATH LIFE

Life is too short to burn out

*"Remember the Sabbath day by keeping it holy. Six days you shall
labor and do all your work, but the seventh day is a Sabbath to
the LORD your God. On it you shall not do any work."*
Exodus 20:8–10

*"A furious squall came up, and the waves broke over the boat, so that it
was nearly swamped. Jesus was in the stern, sleeping on a cushion."*
Mark 4:37–38

In spring 1992, I nearly had a nervous breakdown. My family and I had experienced two evacuations from the DR Congo in fall 1991, both caused by political unrest—and after that we dealt with emergency health issues related to my wife Julie's pregnancy. When we came home that spring, I noticed strange things happening to me. I teared up and began crying at inappropriate times, times when I wasn't feeling sadness or any other emotion that should have triggered tears. Even more strange, I didn't want to be around people. That was out of character for me. During our first furlough, three years earlier, I had loved traveling to churches, presenting about the work in the DR Congo, but this time I didn't want to be around anyone, let alone speak in front of people. I began to ask myself: *What is wrong with you?*

The summer after returning from the Congo, my wife and I attended an interpersonal skills seminar in Dallas, Texas, sponsored by Wycliffe Bible Translators. I learned some valuable lessons about dealing with stress from one of Wycliffe's counselors, Dr. Ken Williams, who had been counseling missionaries for three decades. He taught us about a stress curve plotted on a matrix that related physical and mental functioning to the amount of stress in one's life. The curve showed that stress itself is not bad. Too little stress or challenge in life can mean too little functioning and effectiveness. The idea is to find the amount of stress that sees you functioning at your peak effectiveness. So the functioning line with stress increases to a point, but if you keep adding stress after reaching your peak effectiveness, the function line begins to plummet, dropping to nonfunctioning states—including nervous breakdown and even death.

I learned that the problem isn't stress. The problem is being overstressed for too long. Sometimes God calls us, or circumstances force us, into an overstressed situation or time of life. That's not bad—so long as we don't live long-term in such a situation. Being overstressed for years is very dangerous, much like living on the edge of a cliff: At any moment you could fall off. We must purposely reduce stress in our life, backing away from the edge of the cliff to regain peak effectiveness, regaining a cushion in our life, allowing us to be ready the next time God calls us into an overstressed situation for a time. We will sometimes find ourselves in overstressed situations—but we should not live our lives in them.

Dr. Williams scared me when he talked about missionaries he knew who had lived for so long in an overstressed situation that they burned out, falling into a nonfunctioning state. He told me that missionaries in this burned-out state usually took one to three years to regain their mental and spiritual energy—and that *some never totally regained their energy.* Those words really got my attention; Dr. Williams was saying that it was possible to do long-term permanent emotional damage to oneself. I felt as if he were speaking directly to me by his warning.

Some say, "I'd rather burn out for Jesus than rust out." This sentiment sounds spiritual, but I think it a lie from hell. Jesus doesn't want a bunch of shooting stars—people who serve him for a short time, then burn out. There has got to be another option—a third way that avoids both burning out and rusting out. And I think there is: living the Sabbath life, resulting in long-term physical and spiritual health. Living by a regular, weekly Sabbath rhythm helps re-create the cushion we need in our lives so that we can become healthy servants of the Lord over the long term.

The Wycliffe seminar challenged me to take an honest personal inventory of my missionary work in the Congo. What I found was not a pretty picture. I had been working too hard for too long without weekly spiritual and physical renewal. For many months, I had violated the Sabbath rest principle, even forgoing daily nourishment from the Word of God and time in prayer each day. I had fallen into the trap of working hard for God but not allowing him to renew me through his Word, prayer, or Sabbath rest.

God built the Sabbath principle of rest into creation. Even the dirt needs to rest if it is to keep producing good crops. A starting baseball pitcher must rest his arm at least three days if he is to pitch at his best. Our bodies and minds need to rest if they are to be effective. Fatigue has only one cure, and that cure isn't caffeine—it is sleep. Back when the WWJD bracelets were popular, I read the story of Jesus being asleep in the boat during the storm and realized one answer to the question "What would Jesus do?" is "Jesus would take a nap when he was tired!" There are times when the most spiritual thing you can do is take a nap. I'm not talking about being lazy; I'm talking about resting our bodies so that we are at our best for the kingdom. The world, I think, would be a better place if everyone took a nap each day.

The definition of Sabbath is "ceasing" or "rest." Basically it means *Stop!* For one day in every seven, we are to stop doing what we normally do to spend a day resting our bodies and renewing our souls. Rest and renewal aren't selfish indulgence. They are vital for effective service in the kingdom of God. Just as flight attendants on airplanes tell passengers to put on their own oxygen masks before trying to put on anyone else's, so Sabbath rest is not selfishness. Rather, it is the health care system set up by our creator. He designed us, and he knows the best ratio of work to rest.

I used to try to have a "balanced" life, but the effort only stressed me even more. I thought of life as a big pie chart, with a certain percentage allotted to each responsibility in my life, everything adding up to 100 percent. But I felt as if I were performing a plate spinning act. John Ortberg, in his book *The Life You've Always Wanted*, gave me a better word than *balance*, when he talked about having a "centered" life—a life centered on Jesus. When you read about Jesus in the Gospels, you don't get the sense that he was stressed, in a hurry, or behind schedule. We see him doing things at a pace suggested by his Father. Some days, we see him healing and feeding crowds of people; other days we see him avoiding the crowds and finding a solitary place for rest and prayer with his disciples. Just think about his response when he heard that his good friend Lazarus was sick: *He stayed where he was two days longer* (John 11). The pace of Jesus's life was centered on the will of his Father.

To illustrate being centered, Ortberg suggests the metaphor of a baseball umpire. We all need someone to call the pitches in our life, ruling on strikes and balls as well as fouls and homers. Jesus must be the one at the center, the one who makes these calls—not us. We don't need more time management skills; *we need a manager* of our time! Ecclesiastes tells us, "There is a time for everything, and a season for every activity under heaven" (Eccl 3:1). There is a time to work hard and there is also a time to rest. There is a time to laugh and a time to cry. There is a time to plant and a time to uproot. All this sounds simple—but only if we continually ask Jesus what time it is. That's one of the reasons why I like the image of sheep and shepherd: The shepherd tells the sheep when to lie down in green pastures and when to find water. The sheep's job is to listen to the voice of the shepherd. In John 10, Jesus presents himself as the good shepherd, saying that his sheep follow him because they know his voice. The shepherd is the umpire: He calls everything.

At the Wycliffe seminar, I learned how the Lord uses psychosomatic illnesses to speak to us. We get psychosomatic illnesses when we are overstressed. Everyone's body blows out at some point after it is overstressed for too long. Blowouts could come as migraine headaches, nausea, diarrhea, neck strain, or any number of other physical reactions. Dr. Williams told us to consider these kinds of illnesses as *angels from God*. They are special messengers sent from God with a one-word message: *Stop*! He also taught us to get rid of what he called "junk stress"—the kind of stress that isn't worth keeping, when the positive benefits of keeping an activity are not worth the time and energy we expend on it.

The Sabbath is God's gift to man, a day of rest for the body and restoration for the soul. Now, I am not legalistic about the actual day of the Sabbath: For the Jews, the Sabbath started at sundown on Friday and lasted until sundown on Saturday. In the New Testament, the believers began to meet together on Sunday, the first day of the week—but nowhere does Scripture mandate Sunday as the Christian Sabbath day. For some, Sunday is *not* a day of rest—especially preachers who preach multiple sermons. But I do believe in the ratio of the Sabbath: For every six days of work, one day of rest.

God doesn't set aside the Sabbath principle during busy seasons in our life. Exodus 34:21 says, "Six days you shall labor, but on the seventh day you shall rest; even during the plowing season and harvest you must rest." Plowing and harvesting are the two busiest times of the year for a farmer—but God says to rest anyway. Imagine telling a tax accountant during tax season, a student during finals, or a coach during the playoffs: "You still need to rest!" Our problem is that we schedule 120 percent of our days, living with no margin in our lives—no place between our load and our limits.

God knows our vulnerability to hurry sickness. Hurry can kill the body, and it can kill marriages, families, and ministries, too. It has been said that if Satan can't make you bad, then he'll make you busy! The Sabbath is a time to set the reset button on our life—a time to regain perspective and remind yourself that God, not you, is in control. Life is too short to burn out.

LIFE APPLICATION

1. What creates Sabbath rest for you? What things bring rest to your body and renewal to your soul? What rejuvenates you or recharges your batteries?

2. What is robbing you of Sabbath rest? How have you rationalized not keeping the Sabbath?

3. What junk stresses in your life need to be put in the trash?

CHAPTER 38

THE PILGRIM LIFE

Life is too short to think that Earth is our real home

"All these people were still living by faith when they died. They did not receive the things promised; they only saw them and welcomed them from a distance. And they admitted that they were aliens and strangers on earth."
Hebrews 11:13

"This world is not my home, I'm just a-passin' through."
Jim Reeves

We are on Earth only for a short while, so focusing on our eternal home will help us live for what matters. The pilgrim life is a traveling life. We need to learn to pack light so that we won't get weighed down by unnecessary luggage. Traveling always brings challenges, but we can deal with them by keeping our minds on our final destination. One way we can get through all the difficult things on Earth is by focusing on the glory of heaven. Paul said in Romans 8:18, "I consider that our present sufferings are not worth comparing with the glory that will be revealed in us."

An illustration of this Scriptural truth once came in the life of my oldest daughter, Sarah. When Sarah was a freshman in college, I asked her to reflect on all the years she had played volleyball since she was a small girl. She had played the sport for eight years—four years in grade school and four years in high school. When she reviewed the previous eight years, she talked about some fun times, but mostly she listed lots of hard things. She talked about all the money spent (mostly by me!), all the time spent in practices, the year-round weight-lifting and conditioning, playing off-season club volleyball, dealing with curfews, fighting through injuries, and frustration with coaches. Her biggest difficulty was enduring bench time when she thought she should be playing. She also found it stressful being one of the only Christians on the team. Not long after our conversation, Sarah got the privilege of playing in the NCCAA (National Christian College Athletic Association) national volleyball tournament as a freshman. She came off the bench and played an amazing game—and her team won the national championship game. When I made my way out of the stands to find Sarah after the final point of the game, I found her crying tears of joy. As I gave her a bear hug, she whispered in my ear, "Dad, this makes the last eight years worth it!"

Sarah's "volleyball suffering" is a metaphor for our "present sufferings" on Earth. I never want to belittle anyone's pain and suffering in this life, for I know that pain can be excruciating and suffering horrible. I have seen a little girl named Cindy suffer and die of cystic fibrosis. I have seen two people from my church die a slow, painful death from Lou Gehrig's disease. Two friends of mine have suffered the slow, debilitating disease called Huntington's. I have friends who are battling various forms of cancer. I know people who have suffered awful abuse of every kind— sexual, emotional, and physical—from their own parents and family members. But after recalling all the horrible ways that people can suffer on Earth, I want to look to the shocking truth found in Romans 8:18. I believe that after one moment in heaven, every believer who suffered on Earth will say, "It was worth it!"

The book of Hebrews talks about believers on Earth who went through horrible suffering:

Others were tortured and refused to be released, so that they might gain a better resurrection. Some faced jeers and flogging, while still others were chained and put in prison. They were stoned; they were sawed in two; they were put to death by the sword. They went about in sheepskins and goatskins, destitute, persecuted and mistreated—the world was not worthy of them. They wandered in deserts and mountains, and in caves and holes in the ground. These were all commended for their faith, yet none of them received what had been promised. (Heb 11:35–39)

Reading a paragraph such as this, which lists unimaginable suffering, demands an answer to the question of how they endured such suffering. The answer is found earlier in the same chapter:

All these people were still living by faith when they died. They did not receive the things promised; they only saw them and welcomed them from a distance. And *they admitted that they were aliens and strangers on earth*. People who say such things show that they are looking for a country of their own. If they had been thinking of the country they had left, they would have had opportunity to return. Instead, they were longing for a better country—a heavenly one. Therefore God is not ashamed to be called their God, for he has prepared a city for them. (Heb 11:13–16)

The secret to enduring suffering on Earth is to focus on our home in heaven. We are aliens on Earth—we don't really belong here. We are simply pilgrims on a journey to a better country: heaven, our real home. God is preparing our eternal home in a beautiful city. The faithful believers listed in the book of Hebrews were following the example of Jesus, "who for the *joy set before him* endured the cross" (Heb 12:2).

A former student of mine named Paul served as a missionary in Guatemala for several years. He endured the traumatic event of being shot in the leg and shared his miraculous survival story through his blog. When he did so, he thanked the many people who reached out and sent messages to him during the ordeal. But one sentiment, which surfaced a few times, bothered him quite a bit. More than one person asked him, "Are you coming home? I don't think God would mind after something like this." Here is Paul's response to this:

Really? Don't think He would mind? Huh...? There must be a couple versions of the Bible running around this world. There is the Bible for those who really wanna know God, how He created us to live, and what He created us to live for. The one that includes Hebrews 11:13, "All these people were still living by faith when they died. They did not receive the things promised; they only saw them and welcomed them from a distance. And they admitted that they were aliens and strangers on earth." I gotta admit, been tempted to read that second version on many occasions, it is a little easier to read. However, I can't help but keep running back to the first version ... it sticks better and makes more sense.

I was very discouraged—on the verge of depression—during my second term as a missionary in the DR Congo. I think it was partly a natural response to all the problems in that troubled land, including extreme poverty and violent tribalism. On top of those, I was dealing with conflict between missionary colleagues and Congolese church leaders. At one of my lowest points, God taught me a lesson during a ride in our mission airplane. We were flying through bad weather, and the pilot ascended to break through the storm clouds. He wanted to climb above 10,000 feet, the height of the tallest mountains in the region. As I looked down, I saw a small village, mostly covered by dark clouds that reflected my somber mood. Suddenly the plane broke through the clouds into a beautiful blue sky with sunshine all around. Then God spoke to my heart, saying, "Mike, all you see are dark clouds, but from my perspective, I see sunshine." I am reminded of David's prayer to God: "Lead me to the rock that is higher than I" (Ps 61:2).

A friend of mine, Randy Collins, preached a sermon in chapel when I was in college. He said something simple but profound: "The higher you get, the smaller things look." That is why the Apostle Paul told the church at Colossae:

> Since then, you have been raised with Christ, *set your hearts on things above*, where Christ is seated at the right hand of God. *Set your minds on things above*, not on earthly things. For you died, and your life is now hidden with Christ in God. When Christ, who is your life, appears, then you also will appear with him in glory. (Col 3:1–4)

One of the first people in the Bible to demonstrate the pilgrim life was Abraham. The Bible says, "By faith he made his home in the promised land *like a stranger* in a foreign country" (Heb 11:9). It also mentions that he *lived in tents*. A person who lives in a tent understands that his or her living arrangements are temporary, knowing that a time will come for pulling up stakes and moving on to the next destination. The text then gives the reason for Abraham's pilgrim perspective: "For Abraham was looking forward to the city with foundations, whose architect and builder is God." Abraham understood clearly that Earth was only a place to travel through on his way to reaching his eternal destination: heaven.

Abraham's faith is noteworthy, for he was willing to travel without a map. The Bible says, "By faith Abraham, when called to go to a place he would later receive as his inheritance, obeyed and went, even though he did not know where he was going" (Heb 11:8). Abraham risked the unknown, obeying God's marching orders without any idea where he was going. He was able to do this because he knew that wherever God had him travel, even if it were the Promised Land, was only a temporary stopping place in his pilgrimage to heaven. Abraham was willing to go on a trip without directions or reservations because he had a pilgrim perspective.

The Bible teaches us that we are meant to live in the world as though we do not belong to the world—for, indeed, our true citizenship lies somewhere else. Henri Nouwen says that we can look at our life on Earth as a "mission into time." This mission can be very exhilarating and exciting, for the one who sent us is waiting for us to *come home* and tell the story of what we learned. C. S. Lewis observed that during our journey on Earth, God refreshes us with some pleasant inns—but he never wants us to mistake them for home.

Today's travelers spend quite a bit of time in airports, which can serve as a microcosm of our life on Earth. The extremes of human emotion are on full display at an airport, from the ecstatic joy of seeing someone you haven't seen for a long time to the tears that accompany difficult goodbyes. Airports are also a picture of the pilgrim life—that of a traveler heading to the next destination.

So how do we develop this pilgrim mindset and live the pilgrim life? One way is to recognize certain things that happen on Earth for what they are: reminders that this world is not our real home. Philip Yancey calls us to listen for "rumors of another world." Similarly, David Faust wrote about the tinges of sadness that seem to show up at various times, even at celebrations such as birthdays, graduations, or weddings. He says, "We may not enjoy them, but we can learn from them. They keep us longing for home." This happened to me during my oldest daughter's wedding. The day was one big celebration, but I also felt a tinge of sadness during this transition time. As Rich Mullins once said, "everyone is a little bit lonely." Just so, these tinges of sadness can be gentle reminders that we don't really belong here on Earth—we were made for heaven.

The older I get, the more I anticipate the next life. I get new aches and pains in my body, but I have decided to use these bodily aches and pains as reminders that this world is not my home. My groaning is a part of creation's groaning, waiting expectantly for heaven (Rom 8:22). Moreover, C. S. Lewis says, God often uses pain as a megaphone to get our attention: He wants to remind us that the Earth is not meant to be our home.

When I finished the very last draft of my Ph.D. dissertation, the document assistant sent it back to me one last time, asking me to change a period into a comma. My first thought was, *Why didn't you just make this little correction for me instead of sending it back for me to do it?* But later on I thought, *What a great metaphor for life! Our lives on Earth are supposed to end with a comma, not a period. There is so much more to come!* Life is too short to think of Earth as our real home.

LIFE APPLICATION

1. What reminders can you put in your life to emphasize that this Earth is not your real home? Perhaps the words "Think eternity!" would be a good start.

2. The next time your body gives you pain (from arthritis, sore muscles, or some other ailment), think of the pain as a reminder that this world is not your home.

3. How can you use the metaphors of traveling or being a pilgrim to help you through difficult days? Do you have some trusted traveling companions who keep reminding you of your final destination?

CHAPTER 39

THE PLODDING LIFE

Life is too short to quit moving forward

*"But one thing I do: Forgetting what is behind and straining
toward what is ahead, I press on toward the goal to win the prize
for which God has called me heavenward in Christ Jesus."*
Philippians 3:13–14

*"Let us not become weary in doing good, for at the
proper time we will reap a harvest if we do not give up."*
Galatians 6:9

Sometimes the key to success in life is to simply keep plodding.
Plodding means putting one foot in front of the other without
ceasing—deliberately focusing on the next step, willing yourself to
keep moving forward. William Carey, considered by many to be the father
of modern missions, accomplished many amazing things in a lifetime of
missionary work in India. When asked to reveal the secret of his effective
missionary work, he simply replied, "I can plod."

In high school, I learned about plodding. In 1972, I was a freshman at a small high school in the little town of Kansas, Illinois. The town had a total population of 800, and its high school had only about a hundred students. At the beginning of the school year came an announcement that was big news for my small high school: A new sports program would be coming in the fall, called cross-country. I was dismissive; it didn't sound like a real sport. All you were supposed to do was run. There was no shooting or dribbling a basketball or trying to field a grounder or swing at a curveball. After hearing about it, I decided I wanted nothing to do with that fake sport. Basketball was my thing—I had been playing basketball since the fifth grade, and I couldn't wait to play at the high school level. Then I heard the rumor: Our basketball coach whispered to someone that he expected any basketball player who didn't want to sit the bench to go out for cross-country. He couldn't officially require participation, but his whispering campaign worked. Every guy who wanted to play basketball showed up for the first day of cross-country practice. Practice meant running a total of eight to ten miles a day to get in shape for three- and four-mile races.

I soon realized that this *fake* sport was the hardest thing I had ever asked my body to do. Whenever I would run, my legs, knees, stomach, and lungs all started screaming in unison: STOP! QUIT! I quickly developed a deep respect for the sport. It was the most demanding and challenging thing I had ever done. Every race was a new battle to endure—a fight to keep running and not quit. Running never became my thing, but running taught me one of the best life lessons I have ever learned—*plod on*. One of the secrets to succeeding in life is forcing yourself to take the next step. Instead of focusing on the end of the race, sometimes we just need to focus on the next step.

This life lesson helped me finish my master's degree. I made an appointment with the professor who was in charge of my thesis project. My plan was to gracefully bow out of the program. I had finished all the coursework, but I made the mistake of looking at the bound copies of master's theses in the school library. To me, they looked like books. Certain that I could never write a book, I knew the time to quit had come. As I explained to my professor why I would have to drop out of the program, he responded with a question: "Mike, have you ever done a ten- to twelve-page research paper?" I quickly responded, "Sure. I even did a couple of those in high school." He then told me that I had a good outline for my thesis, advising me to stop thinking about writing a book. I need only to take the writing one chapter at a time, treating each chapter as a short research paper. Suddenly I began to believe that I could do it. Later, when I started another academic journey, this time toward a Ph.D., I created a new meaning for the letters P.H.D. To me, they stood for *plod hard daily!* Seven years of reading textbooks, writing papers, and attending classes was accomplished only by daily plodding. The director of the doctoral program, Dr. Robert Priest, warned us, on more than one occasion, "Getting a Ph.D. is a lengthy process in delayed gratification." We learn the same lesson from the ant in Scripture:

Go to the ant, you sluggard; consider its ways and be wise! It has no commander, no overseer or ruler, yet it stores its provisions in summer and gathers its food at harvest. (Prov 6:6–8)

Another key to the plodding life comes from having companions along the way who encourage you to keep going. When I ran cross-country races in high school, my dad always positioned himself during the race where he could see me multiple times over its course. Then he encouraged me, yelling, "You can do it Mike! Keep it up! Keep putting one foot in front of the other!"

The ultimate encouragement to keep plodding in life comes by looking at Jesus. The writer of Hebrews says,

Let us fix our eyes on Jesus, the author and perfecter of our faith, who for the joy set before him endured the cross, scorning its shame, and sat down at the right hand of the throne of God. Consider him who endured such opposition from sinful men, so that you will not grow weary and lose heart. (Heb 12:2–3)

That verse reminds me of a poster I put on my bedroom wall when I was a boy. It showed a dejected football player sitting on the sidelines of a game and was captioned "I quit!" In one of the lower corners was a silhouette of Jesus Christ on the cross, with the words "I didn't!"

Sometimes the inspiration to keep on plodding comes from looking at the life of someone who has suffered much but who still somehow finds a way to keep going. My Aunt Francie's life was changed dramatically when she was 21 years old, when a driver who was passing another car on a hill ran into my aunt's car head-on. She barely survived the crash and was in a coma for fourteen weeks. She underwent dozens of surgeries. Although her brain eventually healed, her ability to speak and communicate was hampered by scar tissue. She endured physical handicaps and dealt with seizures her whole life. She recently passed on to her heavenly reward but back in 2004, she sent me a card to encourage me. It read, in part,

Our Lord's return has to be even sooner than we can think. Stay on the job, Mike. When do we quit? When we die that's when. Others need to know God cares for us ... our world needs help ... We need him now.

I have been encouraged and inspired to keep plodding in life because of the example of my Aunt Francie, who could have chosen to give up on life many years ago.

Some things in life threaten to overwhelm us. But how do you eat an elephant? One bite at a time. Similarly, Jesus told us to live our lives one day at a time. We need to walk with Jesus one step at a time. Starting a race is easy, but keeping going—plodding on to the very end—is another thing entirely. My basketball coaches in grade school, high school, and college all told me the same thing: The mark of a great team is how they play in the final minutes of the game, not in the first few minutes of the game, when everyone is fresh. The key is shooting well and playing aggressive defense at the end of the game, when your legs are tired and you are tempted to slow down. It's the same in running a long-distance race: Anyone can do well during the first mile, but it's what you do during the fourth mile (for cross-country runners) or the twenty-sixth mile (for marathon runners) that is most important. It's not about starting; it's about enduring and finishing—about learning to plod.

At a church in Toronto, I met a blind brother in Christ who told me of his ministry to people in the AIDS ward of a city hospital. His first objective with AIDS patients was to help them undergo a paradigm shift. He wanted them to stop thinking (and saying) "I'm dying of AIDS"—replacing it with "I'm living with AIDS." Whenever he was successful in facilitating this shift, he was able to help people get on with the business of plodding on in daily life rather than sitting and moping. I will never forget the proclamation of a young woman from Africa who was HIV-positive, whom I heard speak at a youth missions conference: "I will not die before I die!" Life is too short to quit moving forward.

LIFE APPLICATION

1. What do you feel like quitting now? What demand or responsibility in your life is screaming at you to quit? (Of course, quitting isn't always bad. Sometimes quitting is necessary and healthful. In fact, ask the Lord whether he wants you to quit certain things.)

2. Think again of something you feel like quitting. What does "focusing on the next step" look like in this situation? What "plodding step" can you take in the next twenty-four hours, in the next week or the next month?

3. Read Psalm 51:10, then create a simple prayer that you can pray regularly to ask God to give you a persevering and sustaining spirit.

CHAPTER 40

THE FAITHFUL LIFE

Life is too short not to finish well

*"I have fought the good fight, I have
finished the race, I have kept the faith."*
2 Timothy 4:7

"Well done, good and faithful servant!"
Matthew 25:21

D r. Bob Lowery, my favorite professor in both college and seminary, passed away in 2011 at age 62 after a long, hard-fought battle with cancer. When I visited him in the hospital just days before his death, he was very close to death and was heavily medicated. I didn't know whether he would be able to speak. As I approached his bed, he looked directly at me, called me by my first name, and taught me his final lesson. He said only three words, but I will remember them forever. He said, "God is faithful!" Dr. Lowery taught me much about how to live, and in his dying moments, he taught me how to die. He was faithful to the very end.

Not everyone finishes well. I am always deeply saddened when I hear the news of a Christian leader who commits adultery, embezzles money, or walks away from the Lord. How sad to see people who have lived long, productive lives, and who have done so much good, have their reputations ruined by a major fall. Will Richard Nixon ever be remembered without Watergate, or Bill Clinton without Monica Lewinski? The Bible records the adultery and murder that David committed later in his life, and it also describes how as Solomon got older, he allowed his foreign wives to turn his heart from God. Paul uses two metaphors in Acts 20:24 for finishing well: a race and a task. He wanted to be faithful to the very end of his life. He didn't want to become distracted from his purpose or to fall down in the race and be unable to finish. He didn't want to leave a task undone or even half done. He wanted to finish—and finish well. The Bible also records the testimonies of those who finished well, such as Job and Stephen. Considering all Job's afflictions, brought about by Satan with God's permission, and under the weight of the stones being hurled at Stephen by the members of the Sanhedrin, either of these men could have taken the advice of Job's wife, cursed God, and died—but they didn't. They finished well. Scripture records that they were faithful until their dying breath.

I started this book by sharing about Steve Szoke's final months of life on Earth. Steve was faithful to God until his final breath. Two weeks before Steve died, he wrote down his thanks to God for all the blessings in his life, including his wife, his daughter, elders from area churches, his parents, and his church. In closing, he summed up his life: "God has filled this 32-year-old punk to the brim with an amazing life." Just two days before his death, he asked his wife, Candy, to dictate a short letter to his church that he wanted read the following Sunday. After thanking church members for their support of his family throughout their battle with cancer, Steve said, "Even though we continue to meet with dead end after dead end we still hang onto hope, not just the physical hope for renewal but the hope for spiritual salvation."

To his dying breath, Steve was a pastor to his church, thanking them and encouraging them.

I'll close this book with words from another student from Lincoln Christian University, Sam VanGieson (mentioned earlier in chapter 21). Sam passed away at age 26. He was only 23 years old when he was diagnosed with cancer. He went into remission at age 24, only to have the cancer return at age 25. Sam married his wife Savannah in November 2012, then passed away on March 1, 2013. I was impressed when Sam and Savannah decided to go ahead and get married, even though their marriage would be short—it lasted only four months. Their marriage was a testimony that Sam was determined to live his life to the fullest until his final day on Earth.

Like Steve Szoke, Sam spent his final weeks and months encouraging others and teaching them how to live. Here are some of the things he wrote in the months and weeks before he died:

I still trust that God is going to take care of me. More than anything, I hope that through this I can do some good in this world. Do not fear that I have given up hope, because I have not and will not do such a thing. There is always faith, hope, and love to be found in this world. You just have to open your eyes and look for it. That's the good news. I am thankful for my life, down to every second.

Please pray for something miraculous to happen. I do not know how much time I have left, but does any man ever truly know such a thing? All I know is that I intend to live the remainder of my life, regardless of how much is left, in a manner that floods other lives with faith, hope, and love, to live in such a way that encourages, inspires, and supports people, to extend kindness, gentleness, and patience to any and above all, to show forgiveness and grace, to share joy, laughter, and smiles with everyone I come across, to be brave, strong, and very courageous, and to shine my light in this present darkness. Even in pain and suffering, something magnificently beautiful can be born. Above all else, I am going to love with all my heart.

I have given my life to the will of God, whether it be a miraculous healing or it be a journey. Either way, cancer, you did not win! Christ is victorious!

I have a loving family and friends, a roof over my head, and food to eat. This, personally, is more than enough for me. Cherish what you do have, not what you are "missing." No material thing will make you complete or whole. I speak from firsthand experience and, hopefully, with a spirit of gentle kindness.

I must say that I've never felt more loved than in this period of my life. Or perhaps, the love, which was already there, became more apparent than ever. My mom has been with me for nearly all of my doctor appointments and taken extensive notes. I cannot even begin to count the amount of people who have prayed for me, wished me well, hugged me, donated (food, money, time, and resources). Because of their great generosity, I'm humbled to say that I have an amazing family and friends. But more than that, this year has taught me that I'm not alone in this fight, in this life. As much as my family and friends have done for me, I can honestly say that God has provided more. I would have never made it this far without Him. I greet each day with a courage and strength that isn't mine, with a hope that isn't like anything here on this Earth, with a love that conquers all.

In his final days on Earth, Sam was trying to teach anyone who would listen about what really matters in life. This reminds me of the Jason Gray song "Good to Be Alive," that talks about living like there is no tomorrow and loving like one is on borrowed time. Steve Szoke was given thirty-two years to live on Earth and Sam VanGeison only twenty-six. When you add their lifetimes together, they total fifty-eight years. I write this as a 61 year old. It gives me pause to think that I have already lived over two lifetimes of two former LCU students. This knowledge reminds me that I might well be living on borrowed time.

Every person has to deal with death—no one goes untouched by it. The week I finished the first early draft of this book, Vice President Joe Biden's 46-year-old son, Beau, died of brain cancer, leaving behind his wife and two children. Just three months before the final draft of this book was finished, our church in Mason City, IL lost a precious young mother named Darcy in a car accident. She died at 35 years old, leaving a husband and two children. Within two weeks of the final book draft, Kobe Bryant, his 13-year old daughter and seven others, died in a helicopter crash. It was personally arresting for me that Kobe was 41 years old when he died, the very age when God initially got my attention about the brevity of life (see chapter two). The question isn't whether death will come—*death will come soon* for loved ones or for us. The question is whether we will let death teach us, before it comes, what really matters in life. Death can teach us how to live if we are paying attention. Former White House spokesman Tony Snow, who died of cancer at age 53, said, "We don't know how the narrative of our lives will end, but we get to choose how to use the interval between now and the moment we meet our Creator face to face." My life and your life are stories. And everyone loves a good story that finishes well.

After my friend and colleague Ron Butler, a long-time missionary to Africa, died of cancer in 2008, I attended his memorial service—or, as it was called, his celebration of life. And isn't "celebration of life" a much better name than "funeral"? In fact, the bulletin handed out at the service ended with a paragraph describing how Ron finished well:

People who watched Ron deal with cancer for more than two years remarked on both his acceptance and his determination. He never lost hope, but he also never pretended his problems away. Perhaps the best summary of his life and death is to say that "he rang true to the end." There was no failing of faith, no questioning, no departure from the truths and the priorities he has always held.

I pray that you can live your life in such a way that the story of your life will live on after you die—not because of you, but because it points to Jesus and his faithfulness in your life. I want to finish well, and I want you to finish well, too!

When I was in college, I sang in a men's choir called the Master's Men. One year, the director asked my friend Phil Rogers to give his testimony at each concert. Phil skillfully set up the audience for a powerful life lesson, talking about how his father had died a slow, painful death from Huntington's disease, a terminal illness. Phil explained that he himself had a good chance of inheriting this debilitating disease. After everyone had begun feeling sorry for Phil, he hit them with his point: "Don't feel sorry for me—we are all terminal!" Regardless of whether we have a doctor tell us that we have only a few months to live, *we are all terminal!* Unless Jesus returns first, every one of us will die. We must simply remember this truth and live for what matters during the time we have left. Because death clarifies everything, it can teach us how to live. Just think of President Harry Truman's words: "No matter what you've done, the size of your funeral will depend on the weather." Don't live to have a big funeral. Live to hear these words spoken by our Lord: "Well done, good and faithful servant." Live for what matters.

LIFE APPLICATION

1. What moral, ethical safeguards and hedges of protection can you use to ensure that you will finish well?
2. What symbol can you use or create to remind you that you are "terminal," spurring you to faithfulness until the very end?
3. What legacy of faithfulness do you want to leave behind for your family and friends? Describe it in writing, and read your description often.

ABOUT THE AUTHOR

Michael Edward Nichols has been professor of Intercultural Studies at Lincoln Christian University in Lincoln, Illinois for the last 25 years. He is also the teaching pastor at the Mason City, IL Christian Church. He previously served as a youth pastor in an Illinois church for 5 years and a missionary in Africa (Democratic Republic of the Congo) for 10 years. He holds BA and MA degrees from LCU and a PhD degree in Intercultural Studies from Trinity International University (TEDS). Michael's greatest passions in life are preaching, writing, teaching youth, cross-cultural missions, and being a spiritual father to the fatherless. He has published articles in the *Evangelical Missions Quarterly* and the *Trinity Journal*. He has written a PhD dissertation on the topic of leadership transition in the DR Congo, published by ProQuest. He currently resides in the country near Greenview, IL with his beautiful wife Julie and his two rambunctious golden retrievers "Henri" and "Lewis."

CPSIA information can be obtained
at www.ICGtesting.com
Printed in the USA
LVHW110802200421
684996LV00002B/271